SEMINAR STUDIES IN HISTORY

Editor: Patrick Richardson

VICTORIAN
SOCIAL REFORM

SEMINAR STUDIES IN HISTORY

Editor: Patrick Richardson

A full list of titles in this
series will be found on the
back cover of this book

SEMINAR STUDIES IN HISTORY

VICTORIAN SOCIAL REFORM

Eric Midwinter

Director of the Liverpool Educational
Priority Area Project.

LONGMAN

LONGMAN GROUP LIMITED
London

Associated companies, branches, and representatives
throughout the world

© Longman Group Ltd 1968

First published 1968
Eighth impression 1978

ISBN 0 582 31385 6

Printed in Hong Kong by
Wing King Tong Co Ltd

Contents

Introduction to the Series

The seminar method of teaching is being used increasingly in VI forms and at universities. It is a way of learning in smaller groups through discussion, designed both to get away from and to supplement the basic lecture techniques. To be successful, the members of a seminar must be informed, or else—in the unkind phrase of a cynic, it can be a 'pooling of ignorance'. The chapter in the textbook of English or European history by its nature cannot provide material in this depth, but at the same time the full academic work may be too long and perhaps too advanced for students at this level.

For this reason we have invited practising teachers in universities, schools and colleges of further education to contribute short studies on specialised aspects of British and European history with these special needs and pupils of this age in mind. For this series the authors have been asked to provide, in addition to their basic analysis, a full selection of documentary material of all kinds and an up-to-date and comprehensive bibliography. Both these sections are referred to in the text, but it is hoped that they will prove to be valuable teaching and learning aids in themselves.

Note on the System of References:

A bold number in round brackets (**5**) in the text refers the reader to the corresponding entry in the Bibliography section at the end of the book.

A bold number in square brackets, preceded by 'doc.' [**docs 6, 8**] refers the reader to the corresponding items in the section of Documents, which follows the main text.

PATRICK RICHARDSON
General Editor

Part One

INTRODUCTION

1 The Background

The sick and the lawless, like the poor, are always with us. Every civilisation has been marred by the three major social ills of poverty, disease and crime, and each civilisation, according to its lights, has had to combat them. Social problems were certainly no novelty to Victorian England. What was new was the social fabric produced by that series of upheavals commonly described as the Industrial Revolution. This was to give a fresh slant to the age-old difficulties, and, in turn, Victorian society was forced to find fresh responses to meet them. The crucial sociological factor lay in excessive overcrowding, that phenomenon which Herman Finer has called 'congregation'. 'Congregation' was the result of an interaction of several elements, all of which contributed to a society in which more and more people were packed in ever extending and yet ever more confined communities both for social and economic purposes (**27**). It may even be that this social change was more fundamental than the economic and political changes at this time. The commercial economy and the nation-state, with parliament the fount of sovereignty, were well-established; increased mechanisation and electoral reform were modifications within an existing framework. But the social character of the industrial era was new indeed, as compact masses of people, geared to an industrial economy, produced an intensification of social ills.

A vivid illustration of 'congregation' was the lodging-house, the bane of the social administrator's life. These tightly packed dens were not only to be found in the cities, where thirty might be crowded into a cellar, but in quite small towns of a few thousand inhabitants [**doc. 7**]. They were the flash-houses for thieves and the haunts of prostitutes; they were the hideaways for vagrants, paupers and social casualties; they were the foci for contagious diseases. They were the delinquency of industrial society in microcosm [**doc. 2**]. Of the elements which produced 'congregation' probably three assumed most significance: the demographic

3

explosion, urbanisation and the development of the factory system.

The population of England and Wales rose from $5\frac{1}{2}$ million in 1700 to 13 million in 1831. During the Victorian era it was augmented by a further 16 million to a total at the turn of the century of some 29 million. That flat statement is explanation enough in itself, for a society would indeed be fortunate to negotiate such a radical alteration without such dislocations as economic instability and dearth, the risk of epidemic and the possible advent of increased criminality. The population, in fact, doubled during the Hanoverian era; then doubled again during the Victorian period. The reasons for this population explosion are by no means certain. A chicken and egg argument has developed around industrialism and population, and the effect of one upon the other. Those who suggest that increased population produced the higher rate of industrialism imply a planned economy; whilst those who suggest the reverse imply planned families. Increased populations do not always produce industrialisation, nor does industrial production automatically mean a larger populace. The countless millions of China or India have not produced an effective demand for increased industry, while, as England's population grew, there were similar rises in Ireland and western Europe without the stimulus of substantial industrialism (7).

A further contest is to be observed concerning statistics. Most commentators agree that the birth rate remained steady at about 37 in each 1,000, but the important figure is the number that live. The melancholy Malthus, in his *Essay on Population* in 1798, drew attention to his belief that the populace was outracing the means to feed it, and many commentators have explained the increase in terms of an improved mortality rate, especially among infants. Some have explained this in terms of more nutritious diets (less alcohol, more vegetables), more hygienic environs (less wood, more brick, less wool, more cotton), and other physical features. An interesting illustration is the advent of cheap soap, leading to a twofold increase in consumption from some 300 million pounds around 1790 to 650 million pounds in the eighteen-twenties.

Thereafter, however, the death rate certainly declined and then remained stable. The first report of the Registrar-General in 1839 calculated that 335,956 deaths had occurred in the year under review—29.4 per thousand. In 1863 it was still as high as 25.8. In the larger towns and cities the rate rarely fell below 30.

Paradoxically, where the population was increasing fastest deaths were proportionately most numerous [**doc. 1**].

The mysteries of the demographic explosion cannot disguise its impact. Nor is it difficult to demonstrate that this impact was most prevalent in the towns. Between 1801 and 1851 the population of England and Wales doubled. During the same phase many towns increased their numbers three and four times. Manchester and Salford sprang from 90,000 to 400,000; Leeds from 53,000 to 172,000. Blackburn had a 500 per cent increase from 12,000 to 65,000, and Bradford experienced a colossal rise from 13,000 to 104,000. London jumped from less than one million to over two million. Urban life was emphatically on the move. In the eighteen-forties Liverpool's cellar population was 40,000, with an average of five or six persons in each cellar. In the eighteen-sixties Liverpool's population per square mile was an alarming 66,000, giving each citizen, according to William Farr, author of *Vital Statistics*, no more than seven square yards each. This fantastic overcrowding reflected the point that, whereas the overall population was rising steadily, urbanisation was accelerating on a mammoth scale. The mushroom growth of all but new industrial towns, such as Barrow-in-Furness, Crewe or Swindon, and the Irish immigration, which reached its peak in mid eighteen-forties, exacerbated an already desperate situation.

In such a situation the paupers were likely, of a sudden, to be very numerous and impossible to absorb or succour; the danger of epidemics was a very real one; and the possibility of mob rule or of criminals slinking into the anonymity of the crowd was equally to be feared. Thus what is meaningful in terms of social difficulties is urbanisation in itself, and the structuring of the social relations imposed by its growth. Any discussion of living standards tends to revolve around wages and foodstuffs, which naturally enough, would affect for better or for worse the degree of social ills in the town. But it is the town itself which determines the kind of social ill (**8**).

The raison-d'être of the industrial towns was the evolution of the factory system; the large-scale implementation of power-driven machines organised collectively. The idea of the factory was not a new one. Just as population and towns were enlarged, so was an existing mode of production to become extensive. The use of power-driven mechanisms produced a technological snowball.

5

Watt's steam-engines were widely adopted after 1785—about 500 were in operation by 1800. With coke-fired furnaces the United Kingdom's iron production jumped from 18,000 tons in 1740 to $2\frac{1}{2}$ million tons in 1850, which amounted to a half the world's production. By 1833 100,000 power looms, mainly on the Cartwright pattern, were in action. Coal production rose from $2\frac{1}{2}$ million tons in 1700 to 16 million tons in 1830, while in 1802 William Murdoch introduced the boon of industrial gas. In 1850 James Young, a Scots chemist, established the basis for the production of petrol, which, by the end of the nineteenth century, was transforming transportation and other commercial enterprises. By the last quarter of the century Faraday's researches had led to rapid progress in the use of electricity. Productivity raced ahead. The spun cotton figures were $1\frac{1}{4}$ million pounds in 1741. By 1787 they were 22 million pounds. In many other economic fields, such as pottery, chemicals and engineering, power was utilised, inventions implemented and factories organised. A significant illustration of the use of inventions is the leap in patents taken out from an average of twelve in the seventeen-sixties to 250 in the eighteen-twenties. Mills and factories became the order of the day. Manchester had only two mills in 1782; twenty years later there were fifty-two. Soon there were also twenty-four iron-foundries and thirty-seven machine work-shops.

The social aspect of these remarkable exercises in productivity is what concerns us here. In 1850 only 22 per cent of the active population of Great Britain were still engaged in agricultural pursuits, and, by 1900, the figure had dropped sharply to 9 per cent. During the nineteenth century, and especially during the second half, Great Britain moved from a predominantly agrarian to a predominantly industrialised society. The old pattern of farmer and labourer or of merchant and craftsman was largely replaced by the new pattern of factory owner and factory worker.

This collective employment of men in a wage structure was to create its own peculiar kind of social distress. The factory system was particularly open to temporary massive blows of underemployment due to cyclic dislocations at an international level, and was to throw up its own brand of crimes, of which machine-breaking and trade disputing were the most dramatic. It was to be characterised, too, by vocational illnesses, like phossy-jaw or the Sheffield grinders' disease (**5, 6**).

This is not to castigate the factory system with a nostalgic backward glance to an arcadian past. It is likely, as E. Lipson has emphasised, that the domestic system was replete with occasional starvation through lack of work, with child labour, with crippling sickness, with fraudulent malpractice and so on. The point is the quantitative difference in social problems because of a changed social context. It is, in a sense, social problems writ large, in that an industrialised society forced communities to face on the large-scale what hitherto had been often the isolated problem for the individual and his family. And poverty, disease and crime were the most prominent of these social problems [**doc. 2**].

2 The Problem

THE POOR

What was the incidence of poverty in the newly created milieu of Victorian England? Twenty-six assistant commissioners collected information from 3,000 parishes and townships for the 1834 Poor Law Commission. In 1832 poor relief had cost the nation over £7 million, at an expenditure per head of 10s 2d per annum. Out of a population of thirteen or so million, there were approximately one and a half million paupers, or 10 per cent of the population. The old poor relief system was branded as out-of-date and wasteful. Each of the 15,000 townships of England and Wales organised their treatment of paupers independently.

Administration varied as wildly as facilities. Parish vestries were sometimes elected; sometimes they were closed oligarchies of vicar and church-wardens or of farmers and publicans; some had paid assistant overseers; others relied on occasional amateur help. Treatment was very variable. Workhouses were by no means unknown; some had schools and some, like Bolton and Wigan, actually made a profit. All, however, permitted outdoor relief, that is grants of money or goods to paupers who continued to live outside the workhouse. To economists and administrators, obsessed with the idea of a growing population gnawing at a much more static corpus of resources, these payments of doles to paupers were a threat to the stability of the economy.

The most famous, but not the only, form of outdoor relief was the Speenhamland System, inaugurated by the Berkshire magistrates in 1795, whereby wages were subvened in accordance with the size of families and the price of bread. This, it was argued, played into the hands both of the unscrupulous farmer failing to pay subsistence wages, and the indolent labourer failing to earn a fair day's pay. Overgenerous allowances to an evergrowing army of vagrants were, felt the Victorian businessman and landlord, not only extravagant but dangerous. Some parishes paid straightforward doles without any expectation of a return. Some put the paupers to roadwork or quarrying, others tried the Labour Rate—whereby ratepayers agreed to employ a number of labourers—or the Roundsman System, with the parish paying employers to employ paupers at fixed rates.

The problem of pauperdom was normally seen in the light of the rural labourer and small-time craftsman caught up in the application of new technical methods to both agriculture and industry. The classic case is that of the handloom weaver. When domestic weaving was in short supply, he often eked out his livelihood with the produce of his tiny smallholding. The dual blow of an Agrarian and an Industrial Revolution robbed him of both props of support and left him destitute. The Victorians did tend to see the problem of pauperism individually, and the beggarly pauper was frequently, in an age in which piety and success walked proudly arm in arm, thought of in criminal terms. They were rather more blinkered to the idea of industrial poverty, with thousands of men abruptly and temporarily thrown out of work by the vicissitudes of trade. Nor was there much sympathy for those other social casualties: the orphan, the waif, the mentally or physically incapacitated, or the aged. Quite simply, it was one's own fault if one were poor.

The poor laws influenced the lives of everyone, in that they affected the nation's economy and its administration. They controlled the only thoroughgoing social service that existed, covering all the ground that the myriad welfare facilities of today cover. Everything, from unemployment and migration of labour to infirmity and orphans, was their preserve, and one-fifth of national expenditure was spent upon them. They were based on an Elizabethan statute of 1601 which was confusing in itself, and helped lead to the incoherent situation of the eighteen-thirties, with parishes supervising their own highly individualistic systems. The Laws of Settlement demanded that, on a person becoming chargeable as a pauper, he should be deported to his parish of origin. With many of the growing category of landless labourers often redundant, especially in the southern counties, and with the temporary stagnation of labour frequently hitting the industrial towns, such an archaic rule caused endless troubles.

The financial side was equally frail. Each of the thousands of parishes levied their own rate and supervised its spending. The accounting system was a disgrace. Only the self-interest of the rate-payers acted as a check. The magistracy enjoyed some control, but it was never more than negligible and often injudicious. Thus it was that a wasteful organisation, operating in unsuitable circumstances, cost ten shillings per head of population, much the same as in 1818 although the price of bread had dropped a little. On the other hand, N. J. Silberling has calculated that, between 1780 and 1831, the cost of living rose 25 per cent, with many prices increasing at double the rate of wages and thousands of people unable now to supplement income by their own produce. By 1830 the gross national income was £400 million, and profits and dividends were going up and up. It has been argued that £7 million for the sole public social service was less than 2 per cent of this grand total, and constituted a mere fraction.

It has been suggested that 'few institutions have shaped the fate of a whole civilisation more decisively' than Speenhamland, in that 'human society would have been annihilated' without such protection against the 'self-destructive mechanism' of a free-for-all economy. Whatever the case, the Victorian ratepayer and business-man regarded sourly a system which synthetically inhibited the pure workings of the labour mart (**9, 33, 34**) and [**doc. 3**].

DISEASE

A flood of government reports were to depict the black picture of health conditions during the early years of Victoria's reign. The most notable were the Report of the Select Committee on the Health of Towns (1840), the Report on the Sanitary Condition of the Labouring Population (1842) and the two Reports of the Commission for Inquiring into the State of Large Towns and Populous Districts. (1844–45).

The second report on large towns included Lyon Playfair's horrendous survey of ten large towns in Lancashire where the mortality rate was unduly high. Crowded towns produced 'large quantities of animal and vegetable refuse', with many courts having an open cesspool, dunghill or midden within their precincts. This nuisance, he claimed, was aggravated by the 'reckless conduct' of 'nightly prowlers'. One privy to forty houses was quite normal, while he found a regulation in Liverpool forbidding the connection of waterclosets to sewers. The cellar population of Lancashire was a disturbing 6 per cent, and, in Manchester, he discovered cases of six, seven and even eight persons sharing a bed. Water supply was intermittent. It was mainly in private hands, and water was usually piped for only an hour or so per day. Playfair calculated that of the 102,025 Lancastrians dying in 1841, 83,616 were under twenty, and that their average age at death was 22.10 years. He reckoned 14,000 of these deaths, together with 398,000 cases of sicknesses, had been preventable, and that the financial loss to the county was £5,133,557.

Similar evidence poured in from all over the country of sewage heaps piling up to the nauseating quantity of 25,000 or 35,000 tons in the centre of cities, of 10,000 people reliant on a single well for water supply, of rain 'the colour of ink', of floors 'covered with water, ashes and excrementitious nastiness', of cemeteries so packed that bones were visible on the surface and fourteen corpses would be jammed in a grave [**doc. 2**]. Sanitation and water supply were the major problems resulting from overcrowding. Dramatic rises in population exhibited the total inadequacy of the services. Using Leeds as an example, the population increase between 1801 and 1851 was 119,000. Allowing ten gallons a day for each inhabitant, the approximate increase in annual demand over that period was from 200 million to 800 million gallons. This was a meagre ration by today's standard, when thirty-five to forty gallons is the average individual usage. As for sanitation, the annual sewage output must have risen in the same period from 80 tons to 300 tons.

This gargantuan problem was faced by a confusion of archaic authorities such as Paving Trusts, Commissioners of Sewers, Highway Committees, Courts Leet, Improvement Commissions and so on. Municipal Incorporation, after 1835, began to have some effect; the Poor Law Unions were to become active in the field; and some local acts were in evidence. But the overall view is one of medieval agencies failing to tackle a gruesome modern difficulty. Occasional private and charitable works helped—like the Manchester Board of Health established by the celebrated Dr Thomas Perceval—but vested interest was rife. A vast array of commercial undertakings occupied the field, some of them sub-contracted by local authorities. Gas, water and lighting facilities were in the hands of private enterprise, and for a miserable dribble of water, perhaps no more than an hour a day, a householder might pay an annual rental of £8, which is expensive even by today's standards.

The emphasis on hygiene at the present time, the unthinking acceptance of the easily turned tap and its constant water supply—elements such as these make it almost impossible to visualise the lot of the early Victorian townsman. Somehow it is simpler to imagine the life of the feudal serf than that of our more immediate predecessors, living in indescribable filth without recourse to the standard utilities of public health. And, at that time, the prevailing medical hypothesis was the atmospheric or miasmatic theory, which supposed disease to be spread by 'poisonous exhalations' arising from decomposing matter. The Victorian medicos were right to see filth as a predisposing cause of disease, and they were anxious to see it removed [**doc. 8**].

Their fears, if ill informed scientifically, were well founded in practice. With death rates as high as forty to a thousand in severely depressed urban areas, the point was inescapable. William Farr thought that seventeen to the thousand was the 'natural' mortality rate, and that, apart from unnecessary deaths, many felt, like Farr, that probably three-fourths of diseases were preventable. Chilling epidemics swept the nation. Cholera was the harshest scourge. The first major epidemic began in Sunderland in October 1831. By December it had spread to Tyneside. From there it crept to Hull and York, and thence to Liverpool, where over 1,500 died. In 1849 it struck again. There were 53,293 reported cases in the United Kingdom, and this time over 5,000 perished in Liverpool [**doc. 8**].

Typhus was another terror. It hit the nation in 1837 and 1839, but these were mere warning signals of the dreadful months of 1847 when the 'Irish Fever' killed almost 10,000 in the north-west alone. In 1837 to 1840 occurred the major assault of a third horrifying disease. Smallpox raged throughout a three-year period, carrying off 10,000 victims in 1840 alone. Despite vaccination, smallpox continued to claim 4,500 dead each year. A quarter of the deaths were caused by pulmonary afflictions, and all kinds of diarrhoeic complaints, apart from cholera, subscribed to the toll of life. The most tragic feature was possibly the enormous death roll among infants. In some urban areas a quarter or more of those born died before their first birthday, with respiratory and convulsive disorders, scarlatina, measles and whooping cough adding to the dangers already described. 'One twenty-eighth', declaimed Chadwick, 'of the whole population is swept away', which amounted, pointed out that astute propagandist, to the population of Westmorland or Huntingdonshire.

One could catalogue the horrors endlessly. All manner of minor issues made their contribution, such as hernias caused by carrying water long distances, or babies soundly doped to permit mothers to follow their trade. All in all, it was a desperate situation of overwhelmingly filthy sanitary conditions, with wildly insufficient water supplies and with outmoded public agencies grappling in vain.

Add to this the particular dangers of life in the factories, mines and mills, and the situation becomes even more abhorrent. Mining and shipping accidents presented the most vivid illustrations of this, but, day by day, crudely guarded machines maimed and killed their minders. Fatigue and malnutrition, especially among the child labourers, assuredly played its part, while inadequate ventilation was often a crucial factor. Pulmonary complaints were a constant in the miner's gloomy existence, and the wasting blows of phthisis hammered mercilessly at the textile operatives. Consumption figures were always high in the mill towns, and each trade, so feeble were the restrictions imposed by public surveillance, had its vocational hazard.

A further horror was the state of the cemeteries. The clergy had an interest in retaining burials on churchland, and, although the number of deaths was obviously shooting upwards, the parish graveyards remained stable. London was probably the worst illustration of this. Bunhill Fields, a four-acre plot, was stuffed with 100,000 corpses. Every year some 50,000 dead were added to London's 200 acres of cemeteries. Russell Court was raised considerably by sheer quantity of burials, and, in many graveyards, decomposed matter and vile stench was the order of the day. Other tales told of corpses lying for days in one room dwellings among families sleeping and eating and of children killed to draw burial society funds [**doc. 2**].

Every aspect of life, therefore, was marred by unhealthy and revolting conditions, the shadow of premature death and the constant danger of dread disease. It was a social problem which must have appeared to contemporaries as impossible of resolution. Many well-to-do people, removed from the more grisly circumstances, refused to believe the details stated in the reports, and several researchers were themselves made violently ill by their experiences. It was a situation well out of hand and likely to have discouraged the most optimistic heart (**35, 36, 39**).

CRIME AND THE POLICE

English police history has veered uneasily between the ideal of individual responsibility for preserving the peace and the need to act decisively in times of violence and riot. The former principle is illustrated by the vesting of collective responsibility, through the Common Law, in the justices and constables, and the latter by the urgent need for military support on occasion. The issue of reconciling effective action with individual freedom had long been delicately poised, leading, perhaps, to a compromise of what Charles Reith would call 'kin police' and 'ruler-appointed police'.

The onset of the Victorian period was to see this fragile harmony completely unhinged. With a mammoth increase in population and in mobility the 'know-everyone' system disintegrated. The J.P.s and Constables, sometimes on a voluntary basis and with their fellows' cooperation, had once managed their watch and ward, but the largeness and anonymity of urban life was to make this impossible. The growing towns provided, on a proportionally larger scale, the same types of crime as had troubled the eighteenth century, and disorder pressed hard on outmoded and ill-equipped authorities. Expanding commerce begat its own set of possible thefts; frequent dire want was a major factor; the drink and prostitution traffics were fostered by expanding town life; criminal tendencies seem to have been stimulated by the degrading social milieu, and there was the new danger of proletarian mass action, with its consequent threat to property.

The early decades of the nineteenth century have been called 'the golden age of gangsterdom in England; an era of uncontrollable crime and mob disorder which threatened the overthrow of all authority'; a time when there was 'an increase of uncontrollable crime and in frequency of out-breaks of uncontrollable riot-disorder'. One writer has baldly called the England of that era a 'policeless state'. There may be some exaggeration in these conclusions; nonetheless, the Constabulary Report of 1839 narrated a fearful tale, comparable with those of the poor relief and health commissions. It calculated that some 40,000 persons were 'living wholly by depredation', apart from countless others who supplemented more honest callings by occasional crime. The problem was a real and pressing one.

The Constabulary Report presented a lurid summary, complete with long confessions wrung from repentant convicts [**doc. 10**]. It suggested that, with London and the municipal boroughs policed, migratory bands roamed the countryside, pillaging unpoliced areas. There were, it opined, hundreds of beggars who 'paraded the whole country, rendering property insecure' and who should have been subject to poor law supervision. Many a lodging house and tavern served as the centre for thieving and fencing, as 'the more extensively established school for juvenile delinquency' and as 'the most infamous brothel in the whole district'. In the country thefts of sheep and poultry were common, and the tenant farms created by the Agrarian Revolution were continually robbed.

Highwaymen and footpads were no nostalgic Regency memory. The foothills of the Pennines and the roads to the north-east of Manchester were, said one witness, 'where travellers feel the least comfortable'. Wrecking had not died with 'Jamaica Inn'. It was prevalent on the south coast and in south Wales, but it reached its height on the Wirral, where female wreckers were known to bite off the fingers and ears of sailors whose rings they could not easily remove. Excise and rent collections were both dangerous enterprises, likely to induce criminal responses. The railways and canals opened up a new horizon for the thieves, and, given small-scale thefts and passage through varying administrative areas, detection was rarely simple [**doc. 10**].

Another new major factor was mob action for social or political reasons in crowded towns. This is normally associated with Chartism, but proletarian unrest was evident before this. During the St Helens coal strike in 1831, for instance, the 10th Hussars had been called out to maintain order. Earlier still the Peterloo Massacre of 1819 was a notorious illustration. In the thirties agitation against the poor law and in favour of factory reform grew, exacerbated by working-class disappointment in the 1832 Reform Act. Slumps and bad harvests turned trade unionists and others towards political measures. Chartism rose in a 'tumultous upheaval', mainly in south-east Lancashire, parts of the Midlands and south Wales. Oddly enough, Liverpool, with its long tradition of political militancy, was not overmuch affected. Although some commentators now feel that Chartism was overestimated in terms of 'physical force', there is no doubt that with the flare-up from 1838 to 1841, and with occasional flickers for some years, the middle and upper classes were genuinely alarmed. Strikes, demonstrations, union activities, machine-breaking, arson, all the possible activities of organised labour were noted by the Constabulary Commission for the titivation of its timid readers.

The system supposed to meet the menace of crime was indeed decrepit. Parliament and the Home Office stood at the centre, often apathetic and reluctant to make changes [**doc. 12**]. The Metropolitan Police had been formed in the eighteen-twenties, and seemed to work with relative efficiency. Sometimes troupes of London police or of enrolled pensioners would be dispatched by the Home Office to succour the beleaguered provinces. In the provinces the Lord Lieutenant, the magistracy and the county yeomanries held sway, but these were frequently cut off from the mainstream of urban crime, and, when it came into their ken, resort to troops was too often their facile answer. Some towns, under clauses of the Municipal Corporation Act of 1835, were obliged to form police forces. In some places, such as Manchester and Bolton, this in itself caused confusion through conflict between the old Court Leet watches and the new borough police forces. In the two cases mentioned, the government had to intervene and organise matters more rationally. Many unincorporated towns clung to the old patterns of a night and day watch, whilst even in corporated towns policing was frequently incompetent.

Some idea of the extent of crime may be deduced from the crime figures. In the period 1827 to 1831 the average annual number of commitments was 17,000, a ratio of one to 700 of the population. In the period 1837 to 1841 the figures rose to 25,000, and the ratio now was one to 640. A study of these figures reveals something like 90 per cent committed for crimes of gain. There were relatively few sexual offences or assaults unmotivated by profit. There was a handful of commitments for keeping bawdy or disorderly houses (there were 711 brothels in Liverpool in 1838), but conviction was remarkably rare, possibly because of the tie-in with landlordism. Murder and manslaughter were not unduly excessive, and riot and mob action did not figure as largely as some writers, anxious to portray Chartism and trade unionism in blacker light, might have believed.

By modern standards there were relatively few of the motiveless offences, violent or perverse, which trouble presentday crime workers. Despite the picture drawn of a lawless, riotous age, it was probably the niggling, mundane, day-by-day petty thieving which accumulated into the bulk of the problem. It can be calculated that for every commitment to the quarter sessions, there were about ten cases dealt with in magistrate's courts. This indicates that, on average, something like one person in every sixty was haled before the justices each year. And, in an era of crude detection methodology, there were probably thousands of unsolved cases and cases never even reported. About one-third of those indicted were under twenty-one, and only a small percentage were literate. Roughly one-fifth were female—a fraction very similar to the nineteen-sixties.

The authorities met the problem with harshness [**doc. 3**]. The much-heralded reduction in capital punishment meant that the number of executions was very small indeed. But otherwise leniency was not in evidence. A fifth of those convicted were transported, many of them for life. Whipping was still in vogue on a heavy scale, and even short terms of imprisonment were served in fearful conditions. The sad fact must be noted that perhaps 2 per cent of the convicted were twelve and under. Cases of children of seven imprisoned for two months were not unknown. Strangely enough, cases of riot rarely led to savage sentencing—fines, short imprisonments and even acquittals were deemed sufficient. Allied cases such as assaults on peace officers and damage to mines were also treated with relative kindliness [**doc. 11**].

At this time the principal national prisons were the eight convict hulks. These were a stopgap substitute for transportation, which had been drastically reduced by the loss of the American colonies, but which still continued well into the century. These hulks were located at Woolwich, Portsmouth and Chatham, with three lying off St George's, Bermuda, and many of the attested convicts were serving terms of thirteen and fourteen years and life imprisonment. These sentences were often the punishment for the theft of single items such as a watch, a pair of boots, one handkerchief, an apron, or three spoons. The logic was terrifyingly feeble. Frederick Williamson was sentenced to seven years for assault; William Maudsley was sentenced to ten years for wounding two asses. The Euryalus was reserved for juveniles. Twelve-year-old William Naylor received a life sentence for stealing a cow and thirteen-year-old Patrick

Conway fourteen years for the theft of a brass bowl. Some hundreds languished in the county and town gaols, and, throughout the country, men were kept in silence and in solitary confinement and set to arduous and soul-destroying tasks [**doc. 11**].

A complex of crime and disorder faced a complex of efforts to match it. In the nature of things this favoured the former. The lawless had adapted themselves to industrialism with alacrity. The authorities attempted to meet the problem with disunited, slipshod and inefficient agencies. Although punishment was brutal and severe, the balance in the contest between law and crime favoured the criminal. So disarrayed were the forces of order that they could combat no illegality successfully, whether it was sneak-thieving or rioting (**40, 41**).

3 New Thinking

BENTHAMISM

The character of the Victorian response to social troubles is an unsettled issue. Dicey clipped the nineteenth century into three neat sectors. Until somewhere about 1830 was, said Dicey, a period of Tory paternalism. Then the 'legislative quiescence' of Old Toryism was replaced by 'an era of utilitarian reform' lasting until about 1865 and presaging the epoch of collectivism and wholesale state intervention which lasted until 1914 and has, of course, continued to the present (**13**).

The idea that the first thirty years of Queen Victoria's reign saw Benthamite orthodoxy grappling with the evils of the age has been challenged. Administrative historians such as Oliver MacDonagh, R. J. Lambert and David Roberts have attacked on two fronts. They suggest that the prim doctrines of laissez-faire were overrun by the enormity of the difficulties, and that, in empirical, piecemeal fashion, first one and then another device was hastily shaped to meet needs as they forced their attention on administrators. These devices snowballed, via a process of 'administrative momentum', into a regular administrative revolution, comparable with the Tudor innovations of the sixteenth century. Anonymous civil servants, flitting through the governmental shadows, almost inadvertently created, by the eighteen-fifties, the strongest state in Europe. On another flank, they see, running in duality with 'blind forces', the pressure of 'intolerability'. The 'intolerability' theory suggests that social conditions became so ghastly that humane men were forced to act. Lord Shaftesbury is the personification of this feeling. There would seem to be some immediate conflict between 'inherent momentum' and 'intolerability', for the latter relies on positive judgment and action, and the Victorians could not have been both blind and unselfish (**14–24**).

Some elaboration of the utilitarian or Benthamite creed is perhaps necessary. Jeremy Bentham began with the proposition that man's whole existence is guided by his pursuit of pleasure and his eschewal of pain. If every person was left free to chase pleasure wholeheartedly, then, argued Bentham, the sum of all such successful hunts would be happiness for the greatest possible number. This individualist view had much to commend it to the nineteenth century, sickened by the corruption and patronage of Hanoverian politics, shackled by the obscurity of eighteenth-century government and law, and inhibited in the world of commerce by the rigid tariffs and embargoes of the Tudor and Stuart mercantilist theory. Of every institution and rule Bentham asked simply 'What is the use of it?', that is, to what extent does it permit or restrain man in his search for happiness [**doc. 3**]?

Some students of political science have suggested that Benthamism has the same inherent defect as Marxism; namely, that it attempts to combine two incompatible elements, a mechanistic explanation and a moral end. If all actions are inherently and automatically selfish, who can be moral and unselfish enough to be concerned for everyone's happiness? Be that as it may, the yardstick of utility made a definite appeal to the rational, hardheaded shrewdness of the Victorian industrialist and entrepreneur (**25**).

There followed the bisection of Benthamism into two main groups. One branch supported complete and unadulterated self-help, believing that unsullied self-interest would produce a 'natural harmony of interests'. The free trade movement, culminating in the repeal of the Corn Laws in 1847, received support from adherents of 'natural' Benthamism. The other branch felt that too many obstacles existed in the arena for man thus to act freely. It considered that the state should play a positive role in keeping the ring clear of such barriers, so that mankind would be at liberty to pursue individual pleasures. This was the idea of the tutelary state, one which guided its members towards self-help and maintained a watchful eye lest impediments stand in the way of their fulfilment. This was termed an 'artificial harmony of interests', and a *tutelle* was postulated, to consist of administrative agencies devised to prevent obstacles from upsetting the free play of each citizen and to tutor him in the ways of self-help (**26, 30**).

THE WORK OF EDWIN CHADWICK

The idea of the tutelary state was the branch most directly concerned with social reform, and its most dedicated advocate, in both theory and practice, was Edwin Chadwick. He was born near Manchester in 1800, and after training, like Bentham, for the law, he became his mentor's secretary, and nursed him at his death. He then threw his considerable, if doctrinaire, vigour into constructing the Victorian *tutelle*. He was largely responsible for the poor law, constabulary and many of the public health reports. He worked for both the Poor Law Commission and the General Board of Health when those bodies were initially formed, and, although, after 1854, he was offered little opportunity to be politically active, he remained a doughty crusader for utilitarianism until his death in 1890. His austere and severe pedantry gained him many enemies, not least in Parliament, amongst the working-classes and on the press. John Walter, the editor of *The Times*, carried on a virulent campaign against him. Apart from a knighthood, he received little in the way of honour or reward, but Chadwick made a major contribution towards twentieth-century welfare, health and policing services. Like many an incorruptible, he was unattractive; like many an enthusiast, he was impatient and abrasive. A Frenchman might see in him the combined gifts and faults of Colbert and Robespierre; an Englishman those of Thomas Cromwell and Stafford Cripps.

In effect, his analysis of the three chief social ills was identical, and the solution he propounded the same. In his grim way, the greatest happiness for him was synonymous with the gross national product. Unimpeded, men would contribute to this as richly as possible, but impeded they were, particularly by disease, crime and pauperdom. This noisome trio circumvented liberty. The synthetic allowance system, by subvening wages, dislodged the free play of the labour market, and the individual, whether employer or employee, was unable to buy and sell in labour naturally. Preventable deaths and diseases staunched the flow of national productivity. If a man died or was taken sick, because of unnatural causes, to wit, hopelessly insufficient drainage and watering, then he was obviously unable to pursue his trade or craft at a natural level, thereby damaging the interplay of the wheels of commerce. 'Depredations', by theft or vandalism, were a loss to the gross national product. If the fruit of a man's labour was stolen, the loss was an artificial deprivation of the nation's allround assets.

Bentham had employed the so-called *felicific calculus* to measure the credits of a person's pleasures against the debits of his pains. Not to be outshone, Chadwick completely identified felicity with finance. Every purported barrier to liberty was evaluated. Every pauper's loaf of bread; every tiny theft and item of ineffective police coverage; every unnecessary day's absence from the factory bench and every last funeral; Chadwick valued the lot. His accounting was tidy and comprehensive. Completely incompetent attitudes and organisation in the social field not only failed to work efficaciously; they also ran at a heavy loss. The Poor Rate levied in 1832 was near enough to £7 million; the loss to the nation through unsatisfactory health measures was over £5 million; the cost of preventing and punishing crime was £2 million. The equivalent of £14 million—a pound per head of population—was robbed from the national larder needlessly.

In each case Chadwick wished the state to engineer a situation in which this would be prevented. The Allowance System stopped labour from finding its free and natural level, by creating a condition in which the pauper was better off than the labourer. Edwin Chadwick promulgated the belief in 'less eligibility'. Outdoor relief would be abolished and the workhouse test would be imposed on the potential pauper. Life in the workhouse would be so dreary and unpleasant that it would be less 'eligible' or attractive than the lowest form of work, and men would automatically be forced on to the labour market [**docs 3, 5**]. Premature death and unnecessary illness were halting the full, rich play of commerce and industry. Chadwick aimed to prevent this by the 'arterial-venous' system of sanitation. He placed his faith in John Roe's small egg-shaped quick-flowing earthenware pipes, as opposed to the mansized, square-shaped, slow-flowing brick sewers. These pipes would bring water racing into the towns to offer the people plentiful, filtered water and to flush out the ordure and filth into the countryside for use as fertiliser. This beautifully logical device should be, felt Chadwick, self-regulating financially and even profitable, while 'decomposing matter', the causation factor in all disease, would be swept away. What *Punch* called the Englishman's 'perpetual bathnight' would allow laissez-faire free rein [**docs 7, 8, 9**]. Crime made

22

dramatic inroads into the exchequer, and stole from the honest man his proper share of the national product [**doc. 10**]. Crime, then, must be made 'less eligible' than honesty by strong preventive and deterrent measures. A preventive police force, organised on the lines of the Metropolitan Police, should be set up nationally, to prevent, by its very numbers and presence, the commission of crime. Punishment, when it came, should be swift and relevant. Chadwick supported the Benthamite reform in the English legal structure, and he disapproved of men like John Howard who made prisons more pleasant.

There was also a similarity about the way in which Chadwick proposed these preventive agencies be administered. Severely Benthamic, he pooh-poohed any traditional reverence for age-old institutions and boundaries. He made three main administrative suggestions. Firstly, locally elected committees should supervise a natural ambit of control. He wanted boards of health to cover areas of natural drainage, or, as in the case of the Poor Law unions, groups of parishes to unite around the hub of their common market town or urban centre [**doc. 6**]. In these ways the interests of governed and the governors would, in Benthamite lore, be most nearly identified. Secondly, expertise should replace the amateur bunglings of archaic authorities. Hence he expected much, for instance, of the Poor Law relieving officer, the police constable and the inspector of nuisances, for, he calculated, salaried professionals would bustle about their business with vigour and enterprise [**doc. 6**]. Thirdly, there should be a central body, with strong advisory confirmatory and fiscal powers, to control each service, and subject it to itinerant inspection [**docs 7, 12**]. The Poor Law Commission, the General Board of Health and the Home Office were to meet, in part, this requirement. Over all was the stringent view of public funds, their strict accountability and the urgent necessity of cutting the rates as closely to the bone as possible.

Others had had such theories before. In the case of the preventive police, the idea had already been employed by Sir John Moore and other officers in the army, from where it had spread to the Metropolitan Police. But Chadwick was to make manifest the theories in the corridors of power, and, with the aid of indefatigable assistants, the theories were to be broached at a very local level, in the watch committees and council chambers, where the economic argument did not go unheard.

Introduction

It is often forgotten now that a vast multiplicity of solutions was put forward at this time. Abolish the poor law altogether; leave criminal investigation to bounty-hunters; let private companies organise sanitary services; these and many other panaceas were bandied about. *Ad hoc* piecemeal administrative activity and humanitarianism, fostered by both the established and non-conformist churches, played a most important role, of that there can be no doubt. But the proximity and comparability of early Victorian social reform underline that, whatever the forces urging for legislation, there had to be a mould. Without exception the chosen formula was Benthamite, often qualified and diluted, but nonetheless recognisable.

Opposition was strenuous. Many shades of political opinion combated the Utilitarians, from High Tories, fearful of encroachment by the state, to laissez-faire purists, scornful of meddlesome dabblers in governmental tutelage. Locally there were not only the hidebound members of select vestries and Courts Leet, but also the self-reliant 'shopocrats' in the busy, new towns who were anxious to develop local government independently. Vested interests, particularly in the fields of medicine, civil engineering and water supply, fought hard, while the working classes were, often rightly, suspicious of the workhouse 'Bastilles' and the 'blue-butchers' of the police. There was, as ever, the deadweight of apathy and mindless conservatism in certain quarters, and the early steps were avowedly cautious and timid.

Chadwick and his henchmen were probably helped by one critical factor; namely the pressure of the problem on the commercial and industrial classes. Not only were they paying most heavily in rates, it was their businesses which suffered from whatever was synthetic in the labour market, absenteeism through ill-health and robbery or mob-violence. Moreover, the pressure was mounting upon them personally. Vagrant hordes might threaten life and property; homes might be burgled and families molested; once underway cholera would not discriminate between master and servant [**doc. 8**]. Chadwick's ideal was negative. He wanted state action to unloose not to restrict. He wanted present expenditure to reap future profit. He wanted to avoid that 'mistaken parsimony' which merely accumulated trouble. The ratepayers of England had to be persuaded, in Asa Briggs's phrase, that the long run was worth bothering about (**30**) and [**doc. 3**].

Part Two

MAIN DEVELOPMENTS

Part Two

MAIN DEVELOPMENTS

4 The Preventive Principle Before c. 1865

THE NEW POOR LAW

The Poor Law Amendment Act, which came into force on August 21 1834, was of immense significance in the lengthy narrative of English poor relief. It has been hailed with praise—'the first piece', claimed an earlier historian 'of genuine radical legislation'; and it has had abuse heaped upon it—'social fascism' was H. L. Beales's terse conclusion (**31**). Its 110 sections failed to include—such, perhaps, was the astuteness of its draughtmanship—any 'explicit plan of reform'. The programme was implicit; namely, the development of the workhouse test which, by its very austerity, would offer indoor relief only to those who were reduced to such straits by sheer lack of work. The Act itself was mainly an administrative schedule. A central board, known as the Poor Law Commission until 1847 and thereafter as the Poor Law Board, was to have an overall responsibility for relief. Its headquarters were at Somerset House, and Edwin Chadwick was the first permanent Secretary. The first Commissioners, variously described as 'the Bashaws of Somerset House' and 'the pinch-pauper triumvirate' were Shaw-Lefevre, Frankland Lewis and George Nicholls [**doc. 5**].

Their immediate task was to incorporate groups of parishes into unions. These normally centred on a market town or other nodal point, and they were supposed to join geographical convenience with administrative exigencies. Each union controlled relief within its area, and it was hoped that large, single union workhouses would be built. This was a praiseworthy attempt to break away from the impractical and ineffective parochial unit, and unionisation and the subsequent inspection of the unions was in the hands of the assistant commissioners, 'Chadwick's young crusaders'. A Board of Guardians was to be elected by the ratepayers of the union, and it was their task to supervise the workaday matters of poor relief, with the help of salaried experts, such as relieving officers and workhouse masters, who were to replace the bungling amateurism of the Elizabethan assistant overseers.

The assistant commissioners worked swiftly and firmly. By 1838 13,427 of the 15,000 parishes had been incorporated into 573 unions. Gilbert's Act, a statute dated 1782, and a series of local acts governed poor relief in 600 of the remaining 1,000 parishes, and it was not until 1868 that the entire country was unionised.

There was considerable opposition to the progress of the 'Whig Starvation and Infanticide Act'. Newspapers, leaflets, petitions, demonstrations and even violence met the proponents of the new regime, but this indignation has probably been exaggerated. It has been suggested that the new poor law 'drove the Northern Counties into a frenzy' and that the reaction was 'the first angry grievance of an industrial proletariat'. Although the protests were real and forceful, this conclusion seems a little extreme. There were ugly scenes in Bradford, Huddersfield and Todmorden, but in many of the larger cities there was little or no militancy. Both sides tended to play up agitation, which, to the Conservatives and ultra-radicals, was the fearful consequence of a brutal law, and, to the Whig, the mark of a degraded and wild opposition. Virulent objection was not sustained for long, possibly because of an improved economy, the distraction of other issues such as Chartism and the fact that, especially after Chadwick's influence dwindled in 1841, the doctrinaire vigour of the new poor law was quickly diluted. Nonetheless, a profound distaste and suspicion was engendered towards the unions, and an anathema toward the workhouse has cut deeply into the British working-class folk-memory [**doc. 4**].

Much was expected of the Boards of Guardians, these motley groups of some twenty or thirty farmers, shopkeepers, businessmen and the like, more from their doings than from the 1832 Reform Act [**doc. 6**]. Select Vestries, elected under the Sturges Bourne Act of 1819, had demonstrated the value of identifying, after the Benthamic pattern, the interests of governed and governor, and many Boards of Guardians worked hard to promote an efficient and, in some cases, a humane service.

The unions, however, were organised on an arbitrary, perhaps overhasty basis, with little respect shown for natural or organic growth. They were synthetic, and, as such, few union areas are still the ambit for any administrative function. Conversely, the parochial and shire boundaries, of which Chadwick was so contemptuous, are still very much in evidence. Within the unions, the larger townships were often worried lest they pay more than their fair share, while the smaller townships sometimes felt gobbled up by their bigger neighbours. Thus neither the minnows nor the tritons were entirely satisfied.

The very retention of the parish at all was an obstacle. Some unions left poor relief in the hands of the parochial authorities for many years, and often the old churchwardens and overseers became Guardians and helped perpetuate old habits. This occasionally meant, in practice, that the townships retained supervision of actual relief. The parishes enjoyed two huge advantages. They owned the amenities, such as workhouses, required by the unions, and they operated the rating and rate collection system. Chronic absenteeism was a further feature of guardianship, and, all in all, the impact of the elective board principle was probably not so great in these early years, as once was thought [**doc. 6**].

Just as the Guardians were supposed to give superior efficiency in the government of poor relief, so were competent, salaried officials purported to provide much improved management [**doc. 4**]. By 1846 there were 8,240 such officers, who at an average salary of £50 a year, costing the nation £407,000, or 6*d* per head of population. There was one official to every 2,000 inhabitants. It must also be recalled that parishes normally retained their original officers, some of whom were paid, so that, in terms of quantity, there had been a formidable response to the Commission's wishes. Some of these included medical officers and schoolmasters in the poor law industrial schools which were organised in the biggest cities. Each union had its clerk, usually a local solicitor, and its registry staff, for, under the 1836 Act for the Registration of Births, Deaths and Marriages, the unions were made responsible for this new statistical function [**doc. 1**]. The Registrar-General today is still housed in Somerset House, and some local registraries still find their home in poor law buildings. Each workhouse was to have its workhouse master and matron, where possible a married couple, and each institution carried a full complement of seamstresses and porters.

But by far the most important group of officials was the relieving officers. The onus of management fell squarely upon them, particularly where the Guardians were proving impotent. They were the making or breaking of the scheme. Applications for relief were made to them; the necessary investigations and interviews were their responsibility; the decision as to treatment was theirs; the actual payment of relief was their job; they maintained appropriate accounts, and they occasionally superintended rate collection and other aspects of administration. They were a silent service, and their history has remained unsung, but they had the greatest share in the day-to-day running of the Poor Law unions. They were not well paid, there was no prescribed qualification and no attempt was made to train staff or ensure an adequate standard of entry. In such circumstances it is hardly surprising to find that the new experts were often the old stewards under a changed name. Bureaucratic procreation was well under way, and during the formative years of the New Poor Law the officials were frequently of low quality.

Querulous Guardians and unimpressive officials were bound to throw a heavy burden upon the central mechanism, which was probably the poor Law's most important contribution to British administrative history. Sometimes the Poor Law Commission's brief was received unenthusiastically in the country, and it was, in turn, enfeebled by its own lack of power. It could not, for example, coerce the unions into raising rates to build workhouses, and thus remained dependent upon local initiative. The instruments employed by the Poor Law Commission and Poor Law Board were twofold. A voluminous correspondence of an earnest, solemn and verbose variety was maintained by Somerset House, and records, schedules and data were minutely and scrupulously compiled. This surfeit of mail was not, of course, enough. The assistant commissioners, men like Alfred Power and Charles Mott, acted as itinerant overlookers. Some of them had fifty unions to oversee, and, with a welter of paperwork and unreliable communications, they were unable to manage even the statutory bi-annual visitations. This 'provincial prolongation of the Board's secretariat' was, therefore, variable in its influence [**doc. 5**].

This administrative structure of Guardians, salaried officers, central agency and inspectorate was organised to create the workhouse system. This involved a compound of two tasks. First, outdoor relief had to be cut to the bone. It now seems clear, however, that the Poor Law Commission's analysis of poverty was faulty. Several commentators have observed that, in the industrialised parts of the economy, stress affects large numbers at a time, in spite of a free labour market and not because of its absence. Workhouses, spacious enough to accommodate massive outbreaks of temporary distress or underemployment, would have lain empty during the prosperous months. The Irish immigration is but one example of much dislocation.

Recently it has also been suggested by Mark Blaug that the high level of relief in the so-called Speenhamland or agricultural counties was not due so much to the snowball effect of the Allowance System as to chronic unemployment and naturally low wages. In both urban and rural areas, the Commission did not sufficiently take into account other forms of social casualty, such as invalids, orphans or lunatics. The upshot was that outdoor relief was never abandoned. In 1846 there were 1,331,000 paupers, of whom only 199,000 were 'in' paupers, leaving 1,132,000 'out' paupers. Of the gross total, 375,000 or roughly one-quarter, were able-bodied adult paupers, for whom the Act was primarily designed. Only 82,000 of these were given indoor relief, as opposed to 292,000 on outdoor relief. In effect, this category of 82,000 adults in workhouse accommodation was the one which alone answered the stringent demands of the Act, and they amounted to one in every sixteen paupers.

The other side of the medallion was efficacious workhouses. Some unions continued to use the existing institutions, although these were criticised both by the original Royal Commissioners on the Poor Law and by the Guardians in several areas. Some attempt was made to trim the number of workhouses to comply with Somerset House's wish for a unitary system, with classes of paupers segregated one from the other, but this had the paradoxical side-effect of reducing accommodation at a time when pressure was supposedly placed against out-door paupers. It was usually rather later, after desultory closures and enlargements, that the expensive union workhouses were constructed to replace such dilapidated premises. They became, in mid-century, objects of civic pride and self-satisfaction, rather like swimming baths or libraries today.

It was difficult for unions to decide which was the cart and which the horse—should outdoor relief be prohibited before an adequate and classified system of workhouses had been constructed, or vice versa? The workhouse test and out-relief were mutually exclusive, but, having inherited a dual system of poorhouse relief and residential doles, many unions found themselves forced to perpetuate both modes of treatment (**32**) and [**doc. 4**].

The acid test, of course, was financial. The general aim was to reduce the heavy burden of the poor rate. During 1854, twenty years after the Poor Law Amendment Act, 12 per cent of the population were at some time registered as paupers, compared with 10 per cent in 1832. The total was close on two million, and less than a quarter were accommodated in workhouses. But there had been a sharp reduction in cost. In 1854 the poor law expenditure was £5,282,853, a matter of some 6s per head of population and an improvement on the 9s per head expense of 1834. Some writers argue that this reduction was due not only to increased efficiency but to a run of good harvests and to fresh opportunities in industry, such as the onset of the railway era. It is also strange that in the industrial areas there was a considerable increase in expenditure.

What is certain is that the Poor Law Amendment Act produced no overnight revolution [**docs 6, 17**]. It took many years to change personnel, buildings and traditions, and, as the Webbs pointed out, the Workhouse Test acted 'not as a dam but as a sieve'. The test and the treatment of those genuinely destitute who, as it were, passed the test were the same. Harshness, illustrated by the dread threat of a pauper funeral or the barely sufficient diets which led to the Andover and other scandals, perhaps replaced sloppiness of management. Assuredly the mechanics of accounting were immeasurably repaired. But, as under the old Tudor system, little was done to prevent destitution or to attack its causes at source. The emphasis was on treatment, which aimed at 'the abatement or removal of the public nuisance of destitution'. The new poor law tended to deal with the manifestations of poverty instead of its roots (**9, 30**).

PUBLIC HEALTH REFORMS

In the field of public health there was no once-for-all statute covering the entire nation as the Poor Law Amendment Act had done. Much of the early work was due to municipal initiative fostered by local Acts of parliament. The emphasis was, of course, on obtaining plentiful supplies of fast-flowing water and the inauguration of schemes for water-driven sewerage.

London, with 300 bodies operating 250 local Acts, exhibited, on a large scale, the administrative jumble to be found everywhere. St Pancras alone had sixteen paving boards acting under twenty-nine Acts. Chadwick and Lord Morpeth, the First Commissioner of

Woods and Forests in Lord John Russell's 1847 administration, urged the necessity of wholesale administrative reform, and, in 1848, cholera added its deadly argument. In 1847 the Metropolitan Commission of Sewers was founded in order to codify London's efforts to solve her massive problem. Inside a couple of years, however, the structure of the Commission changed, and a political struggle ensued with the General Board of Health, with the lately formed democratic parish vestries of London battling with both bodies. With a thousand corpses being weekly crushed into the graveyards [**doc. 2**], with half London's population supplied with water from a reach of the Thames into which over 200 sewers fed, the debate continued. By the mid-fifties, the phalanx of metropolitan vested interests were successful in halting the thoroughgoing schemes of Chadwick, and the dreadful conditions in which Londoners existed were little changed. The foetid squalor of the city was underwritten even by such a graphic pen as that of Dickens. Such was the noisome horror of London life that its delineation in print was regarded as censorable, and newspapers carrying extracts from government reports were sometimes branded as tantamount to obscene [**doc. 8**].

The northern cities were also making private statutory arrangements. The Manchester Corporation had been recently formed in 1838, and in 1844 the Manchester Police Regulation Act argued that, as the present powers were 'defective and insufficient', wide-ranging authority had to be sought. This was the first of a whole crop of Improvement Acts which attempted to put the sanitation of 'the shock city of the eighteen-forties' to rights. Manchester's first town clerk, John Heron, was as enthusiastic for health reform as he was for others of the corporation's ventures, and national figures, like Richard Cobden, gave their support. In 1847 Manchester began the gigantic Longdendale water scheme, at a cost of some £650,000. The private Manchester and Salford Water Company had rarely managed to find 2 million gallons a day; Longdendale planned to provide 30 million gallons. By 1862 the water-works were solvent, despite financial and engineering embarrassment. Sewage waited on sufficient water, and, for many years, over a hundred scavengers worked hard at removing ordure and night-soil, for which they were paid by the ton.

Manchester's great Merseyside neighbour introduced the first comprehensive health legislation passed in England. The 1846 Liverpool Sanitary Act made the town council responsible for drainage, paving, sewerage and cleansing and has been called 'a decisive stage in the development both of public health and municipal government'. Dr W. H. Duncan was the first Medical Officer of Health ever permanently appointed, and, along with the newly formed Health Committee, he led the attack on 'the unhealthiest town in England'. In 1847 the city purchased the two water companies then trading in Liverpool. There followed an almost legendary battle between the Pikists and Anti-Pikists, thus labelled according to their preference for a huge scheme based on Rivington Pike. The Pikists were successful, and, by 1857, 3,000 million gallons were stored at Rivington. Daily consumption *per capita* sprang from 8 gallons in 1846 to 29 gallons in 1861. The city engineer, John Newlands, began an ambitious sewering enterprise in 1848, but it was 1872 before 'the victory of the water closet was now assured'.

There were several Boroughs which followed the example of the larger cities, but there was an urgent need for a general Act. After years of agitation and campaigning the Public Health Act of 1848 was eventually passed, of which it has been said that 'no moment in the world's history has been more significant'. It certainly laid the foundation for the extensive public health structure of today, but its immediate impact was less notable. Save where the death rate was inordinately high, it was permissive. It was available to townships where one-tenth of the ratepayers so wished, and it enabled local boards of health to be set up. Similar bodies had been formed temporarily during the cholera scare of the early thirties, but the new boards were, of course, permanent. The local boards were either specially elected or, in municipal boroughs, identical with the council. The legal costs of establishment was more or less £100, as opposed to the £2,000 normally required for a private bill. Forty comprehensive clauses guided the work of the boards, which were supervised by the General Board of Health. Inevitably, Edwin Chadwick was its paid Commissioner, with Lord Morpeth and the famous Lord Shaftesbury its other members (**36**).

The boards took some time to become established, partly because local initiative was required to start the ball rolling. Sometimes a local celebrity—a magistrate, a successful businessman or even an M.P.—would begin the process. Occasionally the poor law officials provided the impetus [**doc. 7**]. The initial petition was followed by an enquiry, for which two weeks notice was given. The reports were published and some proved to be minor bestsellers. They posed the Benthamite case in miniature, demonstrating how drainage would 'secure health with commercial prosperity'. After a month's respite there was, where opposition proved serious, a supplemental report, and then, after a draft order, there came the final order and the complex electoral procedure to set in motion another 'bulwark for the unprotected'.

The boards were normally twelve in membership, and, given local initiative, it usually meant that there was an earnest enthusiasm lacking in some Boards of Guardians. Even with such small numbers, tiny subcommittees were formed, and invariably ardent reformers were able to wield real power. Nonetheless, there was outright opposition. The 'dirty' party would try to outvote the 'clean' party, and deliberately stall in the face of statutory obligations [**doc. 7**].

The boards had to appoint full-time officials. Again, as with the poor law, their performance was unsatisfactory, and there was a considerable use of pluralism. The same man would sometimes be surveyor, inspector of nuisance, rate collector and general clerk. This was done for obvious parsimonious reasons, but also because it was preferable to have one sound rather than several unsound officers. But the worst feature of the Act was the lack of insistence on Medical Officers of Health, and by 1855 only about thirty had been appointed. The General Board of Health did its best to elucidate the situation, and in its first five years it mailed no less than 100,000 items of correspondence [**doc. 7**]. It was, however, subject to constant political buffetings, and in 1854 it was placed on a basis of close parliamentary supervision and annual renewal. Edwin Chadwick was rather unceremoniously pushed out of office, and the Board's teeth lost some of their sharpness. There was some on-the-spot inspection, but the major feature of central control lay in the loan-sanction clause, by which borrowing was closely watched by the General Board. Chadwick used it as a lever to press for his own style of sewerage technology, and, much to the chagrin of some civil engineers, there were numerous cases of plans suggested by Board inspectors being implemented by the same inspectors in their private capacity.

Legal and financial difficulties and objections slowed down the work of the boards, once committed to certain schemes of improvement, obstacles still abounded. Precious few boards completed major works in the first five years of the Act's existence. Some were interested in extraneous activities; some seaside boards, for example, seemed keener on building promenades and licensing bathing-machines or donkeys than in sewage schemes [**doc. 16**]. There were all kinds of lengthy negotiations and hesitant plans, together with a shortage of surveyors and other experts. Civil engineering was still a rough-and-ready science; the new techniques and principles of draining, sewering and water supply were as yet not fully mastered. Schemes were badly programmed and underestimated; contractors were a constant source of worry, with their tardy, shoddy and even deceitful ways. Drainage schemes could not be built in a day [**doc. 9**].

It is difficult to ignore the conclusion that, in practice, the 1848 Act was a failure. By 1854 only 182 boards had been formed, and only thirteen had completed sewerage and watering works. Several gaps were filled by local acts, but the picture was a dreary one. In 1858 the Local Government Act superseded the emasculated General Board. The practice of setting up Local Boards continued, but the duties of the General Board were distributed among the Home Office, the Poor Law Office and the Privy Council [**docs 9, 16**].

This is the era of Sir John Simon who in 1848 became London's first Medical Officer of Health and who, in 1855, became Medical Officer to the General Board of Health and thus began his notable career of national medical influence. With great tact and professional skill, he followed up the work of Chadwick, Morpeth and Shaftesbury, and began his assiduous efforts to create a healthy Britain. There is a difference of opinion between S. E. Finer, Chadwick's biographer, and Royston Lambert, Simon's biographer, about the twenty years after 1854. Finer sees them as decades of drift and apathy after Chadwick's sterling if irritating work; Lambert views them as years in which Simon quietly but efficiently consolidated the position with an effective scheme of compulsory vaccination an important example (**17, 18**).

Whatever the balance of progress between the eighteen-forties and eighteen-sixties, there is little doubt that public health barely held its own with a cumulative problem. In 1858 Lord Goschen complained that there was 'a chaos as regards authorities, a chaos as regards rates, and a worst chaos of all as regards areas', and the Royal Commission of 1869 echoed this viewpoint in concluding that 'the English public health system of the sixties was thus chiefly characterised by not being a system at all'. Medical statisticians like William Farr and E. H. Greenbrow underlined Simon's oft-quoted dictum that sanitary neglect was a false economy. Cholera raged in 1866, and the annual death rate was well over 20 per 1,000 in the late sixties.

Awareness of the problem was one aspect; willingness to act was another, and one that made itself less manifest; yet another aspect was the wherewithal. The sheer material needs of the situation were weighty indeed. Dozens of reservoirs, mile after mile of sewers and water pipes, thousands of water closets, taps and wash basins, new hospitals and cemeteries—the catalogue of essentials was unending. Given a labyrinth of authorities and a batch of private interests; given a basically misleading theory of disease; given a health problem undermining not only urban society but rural areas as well, to say nothing of the toll of industrial, seagoing and—as demonstrated by the Crimean War—military life; given unreliable and badly trained doctors and nurses: the disarray of the United Kingdom in terms of health is disconcertingly apparent (**39**).

The early Victorian approach was a negative one. Its object was to release man from the thrall of disease in order that he might produce efficiently. In attempting thus to prevent nuisance, it failed lamentably to attack the roots of ill-health positively. It was a defensive action on the whole, clearing obstacles as they appeared, trying to ensure liberty and unwilling to sacrifice or thwart it in the interests of good health. The prime illustration is housing. Wretched residential conditions were obviously a key factor in the continuation of ill-health. The tutelary state might teach and persuade; it might even encroach with its cisterns and wash basins; but it was almost incapable of thinking in terms of widespread demolition or schemes for municipal housing. The public health movement before 1865 was piecemeal in its success, and its success was not everywhere deep-rooted (**9, 30**).

THE NEW POLICE FORCES

The breakthrough in police reform occurred, of course, with the creation of the Metropolitan Police in 1829, a few years before the chief reforms in either provincial police administration or poor law and health matters. The first Commissioner of Police was a young officer, Charles Rowan, allegedly greatly influenced by Sir John Moore, who had advocated a preventive and not a punitive approach to military crime. With the aid of an Irish barrister, Richard Mayne, he insisted that 'the principal object to be attained is the prevention of crime', and, discarding the disciplinarian models of Fouché's French gendarmerie and the Irish and Scots constabularies, he quickly built up a preventive force of over 3,000, albeit divided on a regimental pattern of beats, sections and divisions.

Charles Reith has suggested that Sir Robert Peel's legendary credit for establishing the 'Met' should be tarnished a little, for he carelessly created innumerable administrative problems, such as the conflict between the Home Office and the vestries and judiciary, the difficulty arising from the Commissioner's power to remove already existing watchmen and the like, and, worst of all, the incredibly low pay. But the Metropolitan Police fought back against appalling opposition from all sections of the community, and, following their courageous and efficient handling of the Cold Bath Fields Riots in 1833, they were more or less accepted.

The Metropolitan force, then, set a humane and flexible example. The tall hats and white 'trowsers' underlined the civil character of London's police, and the rigorous paramilitarism still to be seen in police work on the continent and elsewhere was avoided at the outset. Nevertheless, Chadwick's insistence on night-stick or cutlass as opposed to musket was determined by his desire to leave each policeman a free hand for 'apprehension'. The truncheon was not less bloodthirsty but more effectively 'preventive' than the gun. The example was a practical one. Between 1830 and 1838, 2,246 officers were detached to the provinces, to the chagrin of the London vestries who thereby felt deprived of protection (**42, 43**).

Soon the example was to be followed in the Municipal Corporations Act 1835. Earlier writers suggested that the Metropolitan Police caused 'a wholesale exodus of depredators' to the provincial towns which further sharpened the need for reform, but more recent surveys tend to pooh-pooh this suggestion. It would also seem that only a quarter of the requests for aid from London were from boroughs. The 1835 Act helped older boroughs to repair their administrative structure and newer towns to become incorporated. It obliged those towns which took advantage of its provisions to appoint a watch committee, organise a paid police force with station houses and other equipment, and make quarterly returns to the Home Office. It is probably more accurate, therefore, to see this reform in the context of highly increased urban populations and the general mood for local government reform rather than as the consequence of displaced crooks or revolutionary fears [**doc. 13**].

It was a slow, laborious business. People were fearful of loss of liberty and even more fearful of increased rates. The Home Office had little standing and influence—few boroughs ever bothered with the quarterly return—and precious little exchange of information, advice and ideas was forthcoming. The limits of local government were well illustrated by police administration, for narrow scope made for wastage of manpower and facilities, and left the links of Watch Committee, police, magistracy and ratepayers perhaps too close. Attempts, for instance, to attack the liquor trade were often thwarted by the vested interests of local brewers, licensees and landlords. So slow in fact was the process that only ninety-three of 171 boroughs organised police forces in the two years of the Act's life. In 1848, twenty-two still remained unpoliced, while some of those who undertook reorganisation did so to avoid the higher expense of involvement with county forces (**44**) and [**doc 13**].

The county forces, which caused this mild panic in some boroughs, were formed under the Rural Constabulary Act of 1839. It grew directly from the findings of the Constabulary Report, but it was a timid proforma compared with the Report's demands for a national force with the Metropolitan Police as its controlling fulcrum. It merely permitted counties who so wished to form constabularies under the command of the justices of the peace, and commentators have suggested that the poorly policed towns forced some counties to act. The response was poor. Essex, with its pioneering chief constable, McHardy, and Suffolk were among the first in the field. Bedfordshire, Buckinghamshire, Cumberland, Durham, Gloucestershire, Hampshire, Lancashire, Leicestershire, Norfolk, Northants, Nottinghamshire, Shropshire, Staffordshire, Warwickshire, Wiltshire, Worcestershire and Glamorgan were the others to take early advantage of the scheme. Three more counties wholly and seven more partially implemented the Act, but, in the eighteen-fifties, this left some thirty counties with no regular police service, with Yorkshire the most notable backslider, having just nine policemen in one division of the East Riding [**doc. 12**].

It was probably a mistake to reform the boroughs before the counties. It left tiny forces of ten or a dozen dotted about the shire areas; it also left large borough establishment of hundreds adjacent to smaller county brigades. The pattern was a very confused one, but, by the mid-fifties, there were 12,000 police in England and Wales including 5,500 in London, 2,300 in the counties and 4,100 in the boroughs. Lancashire had by far the largest county brigade with over 500, with Staffordshire and Gloucestershire with about 250 each. The biggest borough forces were Liverpool (at most 900) Manchester (450) Birmingham (320) and Bristol (250). Sheffield, Hull and Leeds had over a hundred policemen as well. The ratio of police to populace in London was one to approximately 450. In some of the larger cities this sound ratio was emulated, but in other places, both urban and rural, it fell alarmingly to as much as one to 4,000.

Chadwick had hoped that £56 per officer would meet annual police costs. The 12,000 police cost £770,000, a *per capita* sum of £64.10s., so that, given changing costs, this would appear to be reasonable. Other money, of course, was spent on combating crime. At this same time probably a sum nearing £1,500,000 was expended on criminal prosecutions and a further £300,000 on prisons—a grand total of nearly £2½m. To this must be added the monies expended on as yet unreformed policing. It was a considerable amount, and, with mounting poor law and public health rates, the pressure on local government finance was becoming ever more burdensome. This possibly accounts for the provinces' decision to emulate their counterpart in the capital and pay low wages. Chief constables of the sizable establishments earned a pleasant enough salary of £500 and more, although in smaller boroughs the police chiefs received only £100 or so. Superintendents were usually well paid, but sergeants and police constables were earning only about £1 a week. The lowest grade of P.C.s picked up a pittance of 16s. It was thought that 30s was necessary to sustain the normal Victorian working-class family, and bricklayers were being paid a guinea a week. This gives some indication of the low standard of living of the police and the fact that they were drawn from the lower levels of society, indeed from the very levels where there was sharpest opposition [**doc. 13**].

There can be little doubt that many policemen were of low quality, and the Home Office were at their busiest in rooting out

40

illiterate recruits. Where did these men come from? The first answer is so obvious it has been missed. There were hundreds of day and night watchmen up and down the country working for the parishes and boroughs. There were dozens of station houses and lock-ups which they used. These were the only men with the experience to be employed in the new police forces, and, in new uniforms and under new labels, the same old faces soldiered on. On incorporation more than one town merely changed the names of chief watchmen and watchmen to chief constables and constables [**doc. 12**]. There was no one else to turn to, but it is patently misleading to regard the newly formed police forces as dedicated troupes of well-trained experts.

Extensive indiscipline emphasised the pathetic quality of these men. Literally hundreds were dismissed, frequently for drunkenness. There were no licensing hours and no friends for the 'blue-butchers', and one visualises the friendless officer hunched for long hours over his lonely tankard. There was danger, too, and policemen could claim little or no compensation however brutal their injuries. The hours were exceedingly long and pension schemes were rare [**doc. 13**]. Little wonder, then, that of the 3,389 who enlisted with the Metropolitan Police in 1829 only 562 remained four years later. The biggest county force was Lancashire, and fifty of her first 200 recruits were dismissed within six months. Frequent sackings might prove the sincere wish of authorities to maintain high standards, but the turnover, in both large and small forces, appears to have been so great that solidity or continuity must have been impossible to obtain.

Wigan provides an amusing cameo of life in a small force, and its early watch committee minutes read like the scenario for a broad comedy. Although advised to have forty police, Wigan plumped for six, and, in eight years, twenty-seven people filled these posts, of whom a dozen were discharged. Fourteen remained for less than a year. Thirty-nine cases of grave indiscipline were judged by the watch committee. Hugh Fegan was admonished because his prisoners became 'more intoxicated than when put in prison', and John Whittle, the chief constable, was discharged for misconduct with Martha Seddon, upon whom he was serving a warrant. P.C. Dobson was sacked for a lengthy catalogue of crimes, which included urinating on the office desk when reprimanded, and P.C. Heath was dismissed for raffling a watch he had stolen from the corpse of a murdered man. Although the weekly wage bill was only £7, the watch committee refused to increase police strength, for, they argued, it 'would be extremely injudicious and inconvenient' financially.

Some of the city forces and one or two of the county forces proved to be of much superior quality, but, given such inconsistency of attainment, it is hardly surprising that the crime figures did not drop as dramatically as Chadwick might have expected. Commitals about 1835 had averaged 20,000. About 1850 they had risen to around 28,000, which, allowing for the rise in population, was a very similar figure. These were for indictable offences; if minor offences, tried by magistrates, be included, the figure would probably be approximately 300,000 cases. In 1849 there were 167,000 prisoners in the United Kingdom. Since 1835 the nation's prisons and bridewells had been subject to inspection by Her Majesty's Inspectors of Prisons, and, before 1856, this was often the only contact the Home Office had with the treatment of crime. Transportation was gradually dragging to a final halt in 1867, but, in the eighteen-fifties, hulks were still utilised at Woolwich, Gosport, Bermuda and Gibraltar. By now, however, the novel idea of national prisons was in action with Dartmoor, Portland, Portsmouth and Brixton (Female) Prisons operating to supplement the county and town gaols. Savage sentences were still the order of the day, and almost 90 per cent of the offences were for crimes of gain (**43**) and [**doc. 11**].

It is difficult to trace the link so frequently urged between the fear of Chartism and mob violence and the reform of the police system. Cases of rioting are rarely found in the statistics, and they were seldom punished as heavily as trivial thefts. The new provincial police forces were not able to withstand massive demonstrations and mob disorder, and the device of calling forth the military or swearing in special constables was to be used even in the twentieth century. The police were probably organised to combat professional thefts as much as to meet the scare of revolution, and, in the eighteen-fifties, they were barely keeping pace with the growing incidence of crimes of gain in the expanding society of Victorian England [**doc. 11**].

The inferences that may be drawn are largely negative. Police reform did not strike in a dramatic moment of terror; it came grudgingly and prosaically. Reshapings and additions were made to the old regimes, and, with crime rates and expenditure constant if not increased, one must conclude that the situation was basically unaltered.

The 1856 Police Act was to change the pattern more radically. It introduced two important innovations. It obliged all counties to organise forces subject to government control, and thus first give England and Wales a centrally ordered, ubiquitous system of police enforcement. And it introduced the device of inspection, already used in factories, prisons, the poor law and education. Hitherto the state had had little or no influence in the police affairs of the boroughs, while its control of county constabularies had been negligible and vague. There had been no inspections and no properly organised central agency in the Home Office, and the only contact with the counties had been a sparse correspondence of some eight letters a year, most of these either circulars or formal confirmations [**doc. 12**].

The three new Inspectors of Constabulary were to adjudicate on the efficiency of all establishments, and, if favourable, 25 per cent grants on pay and clothing were forthcoming. The latter innovation was used as a lever to help the former, for all boroughs with populations of less than 5,000 had either to merge with the counties or receive no grants. The character of this reform is, despite its timing, more typical of the last quarter of the century, and, as it was then that it made itself felt, discussion of its effects will be postponed. Suffice it to say here that 120 of the 239 establishments (59 county forces and 178 borough forces) inspected in 1857 were branded 'inefficient' (**46**).

As well as changes in organisation there were changes in methodology. Prevention was not enough, and very soon police work turned to detection as a principal theme. The famous C.I.D. was started with eight men in 1842, and some city and county forces were to establish plain clothes groups soon afterwards. We are so accustomed to this aspect of police activity that we forget that several, then and since, have regarded this move away from an emphasis on prevention as a retrograde step. Chadwick and the Benthamites had naïvely expected crime to vanish almost completely as the preventive police consolidated its deterrent presence throughout the land. The police were insufficiently competent and the roots of crime much too complex for this to occur (**30, 40, 41**).

5 Collectivism and Consolidation c. 1865—1901

THE COLLECTIVIST STATE

The great legal commentator, A. V. Dicey, argued that the period of Utilitarian reform was replaced by a phase of extensive state intervention after 1865. His opponents have suggested that the legislative activity in the period before 1865, coupled with tremendous zeal on the part of civil servants, already amounted to an 'administrative revolution' by that date (**13**).

In the three fields of poverty, disease and crime, however, this 'revolution' had accomplished relatively little in practice. On the one hand, the services in action before reform were possibly more effective than is sometimes believed. On the other hand, because administration eventually becomes a question of human quality, there was an enormous amount of continuity in terms of personnel, methods and techniques. For a variety of reasons, the new reforms did not 'bite' deeply until about 1860, and one could argue that Dicey was right by accident; namely, the state intervened in theory, but it failed to work out in practice. By far the most important element in this social continuum was the fact that the problem did not stand still long enough to be identified and treated. 'Congregation' was on the march.

By the eighteen-sixties the population of England and Wales had been boosted by a further five million since the accession of Queen Victoria. Again the large towns showed a disproportionate increase, reflected most dramatically in the Irish migrations into Liverpool in the forties. The dilatory and flimsy schemes elaborated by the early Victorians did little more than hold their own with the widening nature of the problems it was hoped they would solve. In a word, pauperdom, the death rate and the level of crime were little better in 1865 than in 1835. As if to underline this fact with harrowing and graphic poignancy, the cotton famine shook Lancashire profoundly in the eighteen-sixties. The adverse effects of the

American Civil War created extensive unemployment in the cotton areas, and attendant upon it came near-starvation, an epidemic of typhus or 'famine fever', as it was aptly called, and then, to cap all, the scourge of cholera once more in 1866.

Gradually the state began to intervene more and more to redress these ills. The belief that state action should merely free the individual to pursue his life untrammelled slowly vanished, in favour of a faith in the state as guide and mentor. Collectivism became accepted as the working creed of English politics. It assumed that each person had certain claims on society to ensure him adequate conditions and opportunities to fulfil himself. Whereas the individualist assumed each person the better judge of his own affairs, the collectivist assumed the state to be. The state, therefore, moved from negative protection to positive assistance. It will at once be seen that the work of Chadwick, whose state tutelage was designed to create an artificial harmony of interest, and the largely unpublicised efforts of mid-century administrators like John Simon, acted as an important transitory bridge between out-and-out individualism and collectivism [**doc. 14**].

Collectivism, like most English 'revolutions', was not cataclysmic. It grew during the Liberal ministry of Gladstone (1868–74) and the Conservative ministry of Disraeli (1874–80). It is unlikely that either, so involved were they in foreign affairs of one kind and another, quite realised what was occurring. Rather was it a pile-up of problems on ministerial desks. As industrial society grew yearly more extensive and sophisticated, the difficulties became correspondingly more patently severe. The 'meddlesome' barriers of the eighteen-forties and fifties were pathetically futile; occasionally they had stemmed but nowhere had they reversed the tide. Imperceptibly, intervention by the state expanded, until, in retrospect, one can judge that the balance between individualism and collectivism fell in favour of the latter during the fourth quarter of the last century [**doc. 14**].

Many themes combined to create the milieu in which collectivism grew. The extension of the franchise in 1867 and 1884 to include practically all working men is one explanation. The arrival of democracy and its consequent pressure for legislative action beneficial to the working classes is of some import. Abraham Lincoln's victory for democracy was a spur to parliamentary reform, not least because it seemed absurd that Negro ex-slaves could vote while English artisans, who had given the Union solid but pacific support, could not. Of itself this explanation is too glib, for democracy and socialistic legislation are not necessarily concomitants, as America itself testifies. Other political features were significant.

One of such features was a tendency for the working classes to ally with what may loosely be termed Tory philanthropy. One side of this strange alliance had been witnessed defensively in the opposition to the new poor law. Gradually it moved on to the attack, principally with the Factory Movement. Here Robert Southey, Richard Oastler and Michael Sadler found common ground with the factory hands in demands for humane working conditions, and, accelerating in number as the century drew on, Factory Acts galore were passed. Although the Tories were not averse to feelings of revenge toward the industrialists for their blows at agriculture in the repeal of the Corn Laws, the Factory Movement was part and parcel of developing humanitarianism, manifest most notably in a personage such as Lord Shaftesbury, 'the complete beau-ideal of aristocracy'. It is sometimes forgotten that the religious creed which compelled him to devote his energies to philanthropy also imbued in him a stiff intolerance. Nonetheless, he tilted at inhumanity and oppression as chivalrously and steadfastly as any medieval knight, and this same benevolence may be traced in many Victorian novelists, of whom Charles Dickens, Charles Kingsley and Elizabeth Gaskell most easily spring to mind.

This sympathetic outlook doubtless encouraged the moderation of working-class opinion, which, in turn, made parliamentary reform viable and useful. After the failure of Robert Owen's Grand National Consolidated Trades Union in 1833–34 and of other visionary and earth-shattering dreams, and after the pitiful collapse of Chartism by 1848, working men turned to the 'new model unionism' moulded by the Amalgamated Society of Engineers in 1851. The craft unions insisted on a social and economic rather than a political approach; they campaigned, relatively peacefully, for justice within the capitalist system; they were no longer intent on destroying it. Collective bargaining and legal protection were their constitutional demands—demands immediately at one with collectivism itself. The 1875 Trade Union Act was substantially to realise these requests. It was only with the growth and militancy of the mammoth unskilled unions towards the end of the century that the workers turned back to more avowedly independent political agitation. During this earlier era they either allied with Tory philanthropy or accepted the 'Lib-Lab' axis. Briefly, the tension between employers' fears and employees' threats had been tempered.

This lowering of the political temperature was due to the dilution of revolutionary fervour abroad and, probably more meaningfully, to the permeation of the material benefits of industrialism down to the lower levels of society. Both working and living standards were immeasurably improving. A lower temperature was also due to the influence of Christianity. After its eighteenth-century doldrums, the church had reorientated itself to more positive social action. The Evangelicalism of Lord Shaftesbury and Thomas Arnold was emulated by many in all ranks of society, while the 'muscular' Christian socialism of Thomas Hughes, F. D. Maurice and Charles Kingsley was also prominent. Nonconformity, now considerably strengthened by Wesleyan Methodism, was especially influential amongst the working classes, and today's Labour Party bears testimony to the continuing strain of nonconformity in English radicalism from the seventeenth-century Levellers, via the Lloyd George school of liberalism, to Harold Wilson and Ray Gunter.

The Oxford school of philosophy also provided a philosophical basis for collectivism in the sixties and seventies. T. H. Green, following in the path of Hegel, the great German philosopher, enunciated the ideal that the individual was dependent upon the community and that the community must secure for him the conditions necessary to live a spiritually full, rich, that is, 'free' life. This positive and idealistic approach to freedom may appear an exalted reflection, but it must be recalled that many who were located in the corridors of power had previously sat at the feet of Green. Matthew Arnold, son of the famous Rugby headmaster, poet, critic, inspector of schools, was one administrator who had earlier mooted much of this standpoint.

But buttressing the political, social and philosophic framework of collectivism was the economy. After the initial dislocation of industrialisation came a juster share-out. This is a comparative judgment. Poverty and cruelty were still much in evidence, but there was some amelioration, helped along by a whole paraphernalia of items like cooperative shopping, friendly societies, railway travel and so on. The character of commerce was changing ineluctably. Just as workmen combined, so did employers amalgamate. Competition bred larger commercial entities and often monopoly. The self-made businessman of the laissez-faire era was partially swallowed into the maw of the corporation. Company legislation lubricated business operation, which increasingly became a question of large-scale finance rather than small-scale manufacture. Each railway company, for instance, was 'the creature of the state', owing its existence to and subject to the provisions of Acts of parliament. Corporate trading, therefore, under the aegis of the state and reaching its ultimate in a national service like the General Post Office, became the order of the day. More and more parliamentary action was taken to utilise the country's resources for the common good, and to protect not only the producer, as with factory acts, but the consumer, in acts concerning food adulteration or railway safety. Increasingly, too, Treasury measures were to be taken to manipulate the economy.

Capitalism, however, also needed protection. The period of absolutely private enterprise was a short one. In the days of the Tudors and after, commerce had needed the military and governmental assistance of the crown to support it, with redcoats to fight the French in Canada or India and tariffs at home to discriminate against foreign competititon. In the early heyday of the Industrial Revolution, Britain had basked cosily in her unique trading position. The Free Trade movement triumphed because it worked. With no industrial competitor, an unshackled economy was ideal for industrial expansion at home and extensive trade abroad. Now circumstances had altered. By 1870 America, Belgium, France and Germany were entering the arena, and Britain's economy was once more under siege. The scramble for colonial markets and spheres of interest quickly enveloped Africa and Asia, and once more there was talk of chartered companies, tariffs and of trade following the flag, as the British tommy sweated it out against Zulu and Boer. Once more there was a move to what R. H. Tawney termed a 'functional' society, in which, as in Tudor times, the state helped control economic action. And, again as in Tudor times, the state automatically extended economic into social action; indeed, it was difficult to distinguish between them.

There were motivations for collectivism in plenty. One piece might have been missing; namely, the administrative equipment to implement widespread social engineering. But Benthamism and the experiments of the mid-Victorian years were at hand. The 'greatest happiness principle' provided a dogma, and the formula of utility was to be constantly evoked to defend legislative action which purported to benefit the public at large. The administrative mechanics beloved by Chadwick and his ilk came into their own. Parliamentary sovereignty overrode most obstacles, and everywhere the dichotomy of central agency and locally elected authorities, the use of inspection, the evaluation of activity by audit and costing, and the employment of experts (now becoming geared to the late Victorian delight in examination) were utilised to further state interference. The reform of the Civil Service, beginning with Macaulay's introduction of examining for the India Office in 1853, was completed by the eighteen-seventies, and this was to have an obvious effect on the integrity and competence of government action. Nor must one underestimate such humdrum benefits of office mechanisation such as typewriters, the telegraph system and the post office.

Local government also needed an overhaul before collectivism could make its impact. Municipal boroughs were again reformed in 1882. In 1888 the present county council and county borough system, through which so much governmental encroachment occurs, was created [**doc. 17**]. In 1894 the parish councils were given a necessary repair, while urban and rural district councils were inaugurated. Throughout the years the local authorities were being armed with far reaching weapons for the upkeep of public health and other vital services. Since 1850 the local authorities had also sharpened their appetite for municipal trading and enterprise, in fields like markets, tramways, baths, libraries, gas, electricity and entertainments. The place of local government in the contest between private rights and public actions was anomalous. Was local government an independent citadel assaulted by public intervention or was it, in turn, the offender against personal rights and property? In the curious patchwork of English administrative life, it is probably accurate to describe local government, at least in this aspect, as schizophrenic.

An interesting reverse point is the slight influence of continental socialism on collectivism. Despite the contention in the eighteen-nineties that 'we are all socialists now', the socialist inference is misleading. The socialist thinkers, Marx included, had been anti-state, believing in 'the administration of things rather than the government of persons'. The pure socialist saw in collectivism, in

Germany as well as in England, nothing more than bourgeois sops thrown to sweeten the proletariat and immunise it against rebellion. We have seen how the trade union movement turned its back on such sentiments, and the characteristically English revision of socialism was, in effect, extreme collectivism. Its most authentic protagonists were the Fabians, among them Sydney and Beatrice Webb and Bernard Shaw, and their Society, established in 1883 preached piecemeal 'socialism in instalments' and 'the inevitability of gradualism' [**doc. 14**]. Continental socialism lent fire and inspiration to English radicalism, but, in its attitudes and practices, the present Labour Party possibly owes more to nonconformity and Benthamism than to Marxism.

Perhaps John Stuart Mill personifies the creeping mood of collectivism more vividly than most. Born in 1806, the son of James Mill, most fanatical of Benthamites, he inherited the moral leadership of the Utilitarians, but had, by his death in 1873, led them across the tutelary bridge to an acceptance of collectivism. He advocated discipline in all that concerned the community along with liberty in all that concerned the individual—a rule of thumb for collectivism which is still a useful legislative yardstick, but whose borderlines are necessarily ill-charted. And perhaps the most dramatic and crucial collectivist legislation was the foundation laid in 1870 for a public system of education. The 1870 Education Act epitomised much of the preceding discussion. The construction of School Boards in areas badly served by voluntary action illustrated the *ad hoc* progress of collectivism. The elected School Boards, with some central control and an intensification of inspection, illustrated the Benthamite heritage. The concern for the children's welfare illustrated the humanitarianism of the 'unconscious collectivist'. The urgent and elaborate needs of the expanding social and economic complex required literate adults to service it, rather than untutored children—the Education Acts were, in practice, Factory Acts in that they prevented children from working. The country not only needed but could afford and could administer an educational service [**doc. 14**].

Thus came collectivism. It came imperceptibly but unmistakably, and nowhere was it more in evidence than in the treatment of poverty, ill-health and crime.

50

COLLECTIVISM IN ACTION

Poverty

As the nineteenth century progressed, the English attitude to poverty altered. The desire to confine the poor law to the aversion of starvation and, if possible, to abolish the system out-of-hand vanished. The association of pauperism with disgrace was likewise modified. It was believed that poverty was the consequence of accident as well as indolence, and that society should protect its less fortunate members.

By 1900 much had been done to diminish the discomforts of a pauper existence. There was no longer any pretence of restricting outdoor relief, that dragon the Chadwickian had sought to slay. Indeed, it was accepted as an integral element of the system, in a manner reminiscent of the charitable underlay of the old medieval and Tudor poor law. In many areas outdoor relief had, even allowing for changing money values, doubled [**doc. 15**]. The Outdoor Relief Act of 1894 went further, for it authorised Guardians, in granting relief, not to consider friendly society premiums of up to five shilling weekly. It was not to be long before the arrival of statutory doles, in the shape of old age pensions, with earnings rules like the 1894 Act. Soon old people's cottages were to be introduced, which Chadwick would certainly have regarded as an insidious form of outdoor relief. He and his associates had regarded provisions for old age as the duty not of the state but of the individual.

The whole atmosphere of Victoria's later reign predisposed the Guardians to a moderate outlook. Their scope was wide enough for them to administer with a laxness which, whilst not conducive of luxury, was alien to the original plan. The workhouse became a refuge rather than a testing ground of idleness. Diets were improved and regulations slackened. The benevolence was patronising and austere, but the days of the Andover Scandal were gone [**doc. 4**]. Civic pride in the union workhouses blossomed, and these somewhat gaunt symbols of local munificence were expensive and large [**doc. 15**]. Preston workhouse, opened in 1868, cost in the region of £90,000.

The poor law unions were making huge strides in the overlapping field of public health. The poor law hospitals, in particular, were making an impressive contribution to the nation's health and to the

51

training of nurses [**doc. 15**]. Behind their barrack-like façades medical treatment is still offered today, at, for instance, the Withington and Crumpsall Hospitals in Manchester. The industrial school was another projection of the poor law which expanded in these years. There was much more going out to meet poverty, rather than waiting for it to exhibit itself. A pleasant sideline on this was the acceptance of the poor law registry office wedding as 'respectable'. It was not all beer, skittles and Christmas dinners for the paupers. The pauper funeral, the fate feared worst by the poor, still left its stigma, for bells remained silent and coffins were not permitted to make their last, sad journey on the Queen's Highway; circuitous routes on minor lanes had to be navigated by pathfinding undertakers.

The poor law and its unions became a much tighter administrative organism after 1860. It was, of course, 1869 before the entire country was unionised, and, by that time, the number of inspectors or assistant commissioners had doubled to twenty. The supervision of audits, begun in 1851, was made absolute in 1868, when the Poor Law Board won full control over the district auditors, and, thereby, over the whole financial mesh of the poor law. Equally important was the Union Chargeability Act of 1865. This made the 'area of administration and expenditure the same', or, in other words, the variability of rate levying and collection from parish to parish was obliterated. The costly business of settlement in a parish —the rule whereby a pauper was chargeable to the parish of his original residence—was also changed by this Act. Henceforward the union was the chargeable area. Thus, at one fell swoop, the larger portion of parochial obstacles to the union regime was overwhelmed, and a less fussy, less expensive and less trivial administration resulted [**doc. 15**].

Outside the poor law the state was embarking on other devices to protect the individual from casualty which could pauperise his family and himself. The Workmen's Compensation Acts of 1897 and 1900 introduced an entirely new element into employment contracts; to wit, insurance by the employer against his employees' risks. Hitherto the employee had had to take care of himself; now the state secured for him adequate insurance. This was also the era when independent bodies like the Salvation Army and Dr Barnardo's were beginning their charitable endeavours. Both state and private activity bolstered the poor law, which, by the end of the century, had resolved many of its earlier difficulties and consolidated itself into a thorough-going and increasingly positive institution (**9**) and [**docs 14, 15**].

Public health

Despite great efforts, few inroads had been made into the terrible health issues of Victorian England. The death rate was still 23 per 1,000 in the eighteen-sixties and over 14,000 (10,000 in London) died of cholera in 1866. Infant mortality in 1840 was 148 per 1,000; in 1860 it was 151.

Between 1858 and 1871 the Privy Council and Home Office controlled the local boards of health, and there was a rapid accumulation of such bodies in those years, mainly under the influence of John Simon. In his phrase 'sanitary legislation with teeth in it' and with 'the novel virtue of an imperative mood' was passed. Bruce's Public Health Act of 1866 catalogued detailed provisions for municipal sanitation and local inspection, and removal of nuisances became enforceable. Then came the Public Health Royal Commission of 1869–71 which prefaced a flurry of activity in and out of parliament. The Local Government Board Act of 1871 drew together the closely related threads of poor law and public health controls. The work of the Poor Law Board and the work done in public health by the Privy Council and Home Office was gathered under a new umbrella department, the Local Government Board.

This was quickly followed by the Public Health Act of 1872. This statute mapped out England and Wales into well-defined districts under well-defined authorities. Many local boards, boroughs and improvement commissions became known as urban sanitary authorities, while the remaining area, which had nominally been under the rather nebulous control of the Boards of Guardians, became rural sanitary authorities. Apart from this overall influence, there was a further significant breakthrough in the compulsory appointment of medical officers of health in each of these authorities.

In 1875 the Public Health Act usually associated with Slater-Booth, President of the Local Government Board, was passed. Of this Act it has been said that 'all the cities and towns in this country have become places fit to live in' under its provisions. This 'model enactment' consolidated all previous legislation and it was all-pervading in its influence. Its proponents urged the establishment of the 'national sanitary minimum', and its comprehensive clauses included water supply and sewage removal, the regulation of streets and buildings, removal of nuisances, food inspection, notification and suppression of diseases, rules for burial and the regulation of markets, lighting and offensive trades [**doc. 16**].

With the general local government reorganisation in the eighteen-eighties and nineties, there were corresponding alterations in health administration. After 1888 the counties and county boroughs became the principal ambit for public health matters, and county medical officers of health were appointed [**doc. 17**]. The urban and rural sanitary authorities mainly became the urban and rural district councils of 1894. The Local Government Board considerably heightened the degree of its authority and the calibre of its advice and information. It was in the field of public health that central authority bit quickly and deeply in the last quarter of the century. There were disadvantages, prominent among them an over-separation of the administrative and medical sides of the organisation.

It was in this same era that the large towns consolidated their hesitating first steps towards adequate provision of water supply and, more especially, water-driven sanitation. It was, for example, 1866 before Rochdale took over the local water company which had left the town unwatered for half the day during the summer, and, in 1868, there were still 4,000 middens or earth closets in the town. It was 1879 before trunk sewers were laid. In Warrington it was 1891 before the water supply came under municipal control, at a cost of £270,000, and a water-carriage system of sewerage was developed only after 1872. By the turn of the century most cities and towns had organised these basic services on efficient lines.

The mood had changed from negative protection to direct interference. Acts governing working conditions and the sale of foods and drugs made their contribution, but indubitably the most critical pointer affected housing. Overcrowded and insanitary dwellings were a major cause of ill-health, but to remedy this was all but impossible, for the Englishman's home was his castle or, at least, that of his landlord. Odd attempts at regulation, especially prior to building, had been made, but it was Torrens's 1868 Artisans' and Labourers' Dwellings Act that first breached the sacred rights of property. This Act went some way to obliging owners to keep their rented houses in proper repair [**doc. 15**].

Richard Cross, one of Disraeli's cabinet, was instrumental in elaborating housing legislation during the subsequent Conservative ministry. Eventually the Housing of the Working Classes Acts of 1890 and 1900 enjoined local authorities to demolish unfit housing and provide alternative accommodation, if necessary through compulsory purchase. This onslaught on a sacrosanct area was to foreshadow the mighty development of municipal housing and 'new towns' in the twentieth century.

Scientific and industrial advance was of considerable help. The infant technology of civil engineering was substantially improved, and the whole business of constructing large-scale water and sewage schemes became, if incredibly expensive, at least properly planned and successfully accomplished. Housing was not only subject to more rigid inspection; building techniques were, rather late in the day, responding to the pressures of industrialism. It is hard to exaggerate the difficulties of the engineers and builders, who were often faced with the problem of wholesale works throughout entire towns, but, gradually, firm strides were taken.

Another type of bottleneck was negotiated during this period with the discovery by Pasteur and Koch of the germ theory of disease. In England the cholera and typhoid bacilli were identified. The environmentalists had done the right thing for the wrong reason. Sometimes (as when, in an effort to dispose of filth swiftly, the local water supply was utilised) there were evident dangers. The true connection of filth and disease having been revealed, medical practitioners and health reformers were infinitely better armed, and communal and private standards of hygiene could be emphasised. In 1865 Lister first used his antiseptic technique, and this, coupled with steadily growing information about bacteria, gave hospitals a completely new lease of life. It was in this last quarter of the century that 'hospitalisation' was to come to fruition. There were forward steps in the education of doctors between 1830 and 1858, culminating in the 1858 Medical Act which established a supervisory agency, the General Council for Medical Education and Registration. This 'decisive turning-point', stimulated by the highly significant demands of a middle-class 'health-consciousness', paid huge dividends as the century wound on [**doc. 17**].

By the census of 1901 results were becoming encouraging and

dramatic. The death rate had dropped below 18 per 1,000 and William Farr, father of vital statistics, had, it will be remembered, argued that 17 was the 'natural' level. Overcrowding was slightly abated; the average number in a house had been six throughout the century, but, in 1901, it was five, and the houses were often of superior quality. The terrifying wildfire epidemics were left behind. The first 'clean milk' depot was opened at St Helens in 1899, and so on. There were, of course, features guaranteed to scatter complacency. There was some smallpox in the opening years of the seventies, and cholera struck briefly in 1893. There were typhoid epidemics in Maidstone in 1897 and Blackburn in 1881, but their restriction to a single area was, in one sense, a triumph. One difficulty was a decline in vigilance as a disease, apparently conquered, lay dormant; for example, vaccinations dropped after 1871. As a consequence it was disconcerting, in 1901, to find smallpox and even plague in the large ports. As a final reminder of the potency of disease, the first of the influenza epidemics battered the nation in the winter of 1889–90. Nonetheless, presented with a gargantuan issue, the Victorians had faced manfully their task of creating a healthier Britain (**9, 35, 37, 38**) and [**docs 16, 17**].

Law and order

It was noted earlier that the 1856 County and Borough Police Act created the framework for a complete national policing system. It obliged all counties to set up a constabulary, and these, together with the borough forces, were subject to Home Office inspection by the three new Inspectors of Constabulary. As with the poor law and public health, a full and comprehensive coverage was wrought, dependent upon central control and examination of local bodies. Just as the poor law and public health were subjected to a financial lever, with regard to sanctions for loans, so did the Home Office encourage the police authorities by 25 per cent grants where the inspectors found 'efficiency'.

The watch committees continued to control the borough forces, and, as the franchise was extended, these committees became, theoretically, 'democratised'. Similarly with the county forces. The 1888 County Councils Act introduced the device of the Standing Joint Committee of J.P.s and county councillors, as opposed to the previous control by the magistracy. It has, however, been sometimes suggested that the County Councils Act was retrogressive, in that it often gave effective power to the embattled backwoodsmen of the rural regions.

Be that as it may, there can be little doubt of the thoroughgoing nature of the 1856 statute. The inspectors were usually ex-chief constables who had earned a reputation for high standards, like Lieutenant Colonel John Woodford, late of the Lancashire force. The outstanding counties produced constabularies with the sudden flourish of the conjuror. Many boroughs with less than 5,000 population quickly gave up the ghost and amalgamated with the counties. Many other boroughs underwent almost overnight repentance, and doubled and trebled their establishments within three or four years. Wigan, which had struggled on for so long with six policemen, abruptly jumped to thirty-two. By 1860 Liverpool's police numbered nearly one thousand.

The inspections were severe and detailed [**doc. 18**]. Clothing, cells, quality of men, equipment—all these were severely criticised in the early constabulary reports, and, eager for their grant, the authorities acted without delay. By 1860 only seventy-eight forces were 'inefficient'. By 1890 there were none, and an 'inefficient' label has been a rarity ever since. By 1860 there were over 20,000 police in the country, and their standard of discipline and quality had considerably improved. The supervisory capacity of the Home Office also helped in terms of cooperation among forces and in the transmission of information. New techniques were introduced, including the mounted police, finger-printing and other recording and statistical devices, and the use of the telegraph and mailing systems.

The small force was still a problematic issue. An attempt was made to reduce or repair such forces in the 1877 Municipal Corporations (new Charters) Act, which denied the right of new boroughs to form police forces where the population fell under 20,000, while the 1882 Municipal Corporations Act enforced the establishment of proper police forces in a handful of boroughs which had held out against reform. The County Councils Act encouraged mergers with the adjacent county where population was less than 10,000. Such efforts were not greatly successful, for they ran counter to the independent, perhaps insular, spirit of English local government. In 1860 there were 58 county and 166 borough forces; in 1900 there were still 58 county and 137 borough forces. This was hardly a promising tendency, but at least the country was fairly sufficiently policed.

Prisons had had some vestige of national control since 1823, when Peel was Home Secretary, and in 1835 Inspectors of Prisons had been appointed to supervise the work of the magistrates and corporations who ran most of the gaols. National penitentiaries were slowly built, many of them 'huge castellated structures' like Pentonville, with its solitude and separation system. The 'cellular' approach, by which convicts were confined alone in cells, was prominent, and its harsh application by Governor Austin at Birmingham in the years 1851–4 created a notorious scandal. As a result of the Carnarvon Committee's report, the 1865 Prisons Act led to a tightening of government control.

This laid the basis for a national prison system, and the number of prisons was reduced from 193 to 112. With a view to cutting the county rates drastically, the prisons were nationalised in 1877, with Edward du Cane as first Chairman of the Prison Commission. By 1895 there were only sixty-one prisons remaining. It was a hygienic (gaol-fever, yet another sobriquet for typhus, had vanished), economic, but soulless regime. Transportation had died a lingering death, but was everywhere replaced by penal servitude, frequently on the treadmill. Punishment was squarely based on Bentham's and Chadwick's 'less eligibility' principle; prison and the other consequences of crime had to be less preferable than the honest life.

But the numbers incarcerated in the prisons failed to dwindle. There would seem to have been some decrease in commitments in the early eighteen-sixties, probably due to the efficiency of the reformed police, but the figures soon began to climb again. There was some consternation at this, especially in view of 'great commercial prosperity'. One explanation was that the end of most capital punishment and the termination of transportation augmented the ranks of the habitual criminal. More likely the spur of want was sharpened by commercial prosperity, and the criminals discovered or elaborated new needs. The seesaw between policeman and criminal continued to rock; the criminal adapted himself to a changed situation, and the crime figures, apart from a spectacular leap or plunge, remained fairly consistent [**doc. 18**].

Public order had, however, been reasonably well assured by 1900. Mass agitation had all but disappeared, although whether this was due to the police or not is a moot point. When mob activity occurred the police were sometimes powerless, and, for instance,

Preston witnessed military operations against workers in 1853–4, 1863 and 1878. By the death of Victoria, nonetheless, only the very frightened could have feared a proletarian uprising. The character of crime changed in other ways. Theft had just about monopolised the Victorian criminal scene, with drunkenness the chief of the minor offences. Towards the end of the century slightly more crimes of damage, malice, violence, assault and sex seemed to be recorded.

As for the police, detection continued to supersede prevention, and soon even quite small forces operated a detective squad. Detection is an indirect deterrent, but its emphasis on action after crime was not in keeping with the original preventive spirit. As with medicine, cure is more dramatic than prevention. A very human appetite for the 'melancholy incident' (that favourite Victorian by-line) was whetted by newspapers and broadsheets, while a massive weight of fiction fostered this craving, with Wilkie Collins and Conan Doyle setting an early pace for many a mystery writer. Thus the policeman, presently donning his familiar cone-shaped helmet, was ever to be a distinctive social feature, and this popular fascination must have contributed to policemen's desire to act positively, detecting, hunting and arresting. Compared with this public image, poor law and public health workers were permitted to operate in silence and calm.

All in all, the onset of the twentieth century saw Britain with a well organised and civic-spirited police system, but crime itself showed few signs of disappearing (**40, 44, 47**) and [**doc. 18**].

Part Three

ASSESSMENT

6 The effects on the Twentieth Century

A description of collectivism in action must, of necessity, rehearse an abundance of Acts of parliament. The key to collectivism was the deliberate and premeditated intervention of the state, through parliament, into the lives of its members. The character of the Acts changed, too. No longer were statutes timid and permissive, leaving broad scope to private and local initiative; they were forceful and direct, their provisions compulsory and farreaching and backed by powerful central agencies and inspectorates.

We have traced the growth of such administrative organisms in the three major social fields. It is as well to add a reminder that they were not exclusive. Similar proclivities were happening in other areas of social administration. Education and industrial welfare have already been touched on, but there were others, such as fire prevention and libraries. For better or for worse, the collectivist trend has continued until today the state, either directly or through nationalised or local governmental agencies, is at hand in every nook and cranny of the citizen's existence.

With regard to ill-health, poverty and, less notably, crime, there have been grand advances. Whatever the success of administrative machinery, however, there is no gainsaying that betterment has stemmed principally from sheer material improvement. The U.S.A., where collectivism has scarcely flourished, demonstrates this point. Conversely, standards rise. The continuation of crimes for gain has already been noted, but it is equally true that one's yardstick of poverty or unhealthy conditions also rises with improved living standards.

The impetus of collectivism seems inexhaustible, and there can be little doubt that the momentum unleashed by Victorian administrators has gathered considerable velocity. In the twentieth century collectivism has run on consistently, albeit with two exaggerated waves. The first of these occurred before the First World War, during the Liberal Government associated with Asquith and Lloyd George. The 1908 Old Age Pensions Act and the 1911 National Insurance Act were the main planks of their legislative platform. Following the Second World War came the second wave, the so-called 'silent revolution' of Attlee's Labour administration. Basing much of its social legislation on the former Beveridge Report, Mr (later Earl) Attlee's government virtually created the Welfare State, in which social protection was afforded each citizen from cradle to grave, whatever casualty might befall him, from help for expectant mothers and orange juice for young babies to funeral grants, along with child allowances, free milk and subsidised school meals, and sickness and unemployment benefits. The collectivist threads already in existence were drawn together and patterned into a unified, doctrinaire format. The whole framework found its hub in the National Health Service, the creation of the Welsh Labour leader, Aneurin Bevan.

So much of this is taken for granted nowadays that it is strange to recall the desperate squabbles over the origins of the Welfare State. The positive attack of collectivism is most apparent on poverty and disease, but crime is also treated differently. Although in 1965 national commitments were over one million, the gentler approach shown to the sick and impoverished now characterises much of authority's attitude towards the criminal. He is regarded as more of a social misfit than before, and strenuous efforts are made to rehabilitate him and treat him with a leniency foreign to the Victorians. Detection—the positive side of policework—is very much to the fore. There was an interesting sidelight on this at the time of the Great Train Robbery. Senior police officers claimed that, so intense was the searching and questioning that followed it, crime came almost to a standstill in the Home Counties. This 'turning over' of known or suspect criminals would have delighted Chadwick.

The Benthamite origins for collectivist administration have sustained their influence to the present time. Utility still remains the 'legislative dogma', the rough and ready criterion for reform. The statisticians and cost analysts who calculate and evaluate the price of social services have an eerie mid-Victorian aura about them. The ideal statute is naturally the one that combines the optimum of moral rectitude with the optimum of economy. Some of the collectivist momentum must, indeed, be ascribed to the Englishman's becoming accustomed to heavy taxation. Taxation doubled from £75m in 1886 to £154m in 1912, and the figures by now are colossal. It is still said that men pay taxes in sorrow and rates in anger. The imagination boggles at the possible reaction of the early Victorian ratepayer to today's fantastic bills, for he jibbed at coppers for the most needy public works. Whatever else may be said of collectivism, it is more expensive in outlay than individualism, and, over the years, the Englishman has become resigned to it. This acceptance has been validly cushioned by the austere approach to auditing and accounting of public funds, inherited from the middle of the last century.

Another heritage has been the use made of the central authority. The Poor Law Commission created this precedent in 1834. It was superseded by the Poor Law Board and the Local Government Board. Later there was to be the Ministry of Labour and National Insurance and now there is the Ministry of Social Security. The General Board of Health evolved, through Privy Council status and as part of the Local Government Board, to become the Ministry of Health in 1919. The Home Office steadily built up its slender grasp of law and order until today it supervises police forces and prisons throughout the land.

The rise of the inspectorates must be coupled with this centralising trend. The first inspectors were the four Factory Inspectors of 1833. Prison and Education Inspectors followed. The Assistant Poor Law Commissioners, the General Board of Health Inspectors and the Inspectors of Constabulary also joined the invigilating fray. Despite much opposition, they eventually taught their countrymen to accept the value of itinerant overlookers in all aspects of social administration.

Chadwick's *tutelle* had consisted of a partnership between impersonal central body and locally elected committee. This again has stood the test of time. The watch committees still have control of the borough police forces, and the magistrates still have some surveillance of the county forces. Much of the work of the Guardians was ultimately transferred after 1929 to the county councils, again as local boards of health under the aegis of the General Board of Health. Non-incorporated areas controlled by local boards of health blossomed into viable local government units as urban sanitary authorities, and then urban district councils. Improvement commissions and unionised rural areas became rural sanitary authorities, and then rural district councils.

Strangely enough, it was the much vaunted union areas which suffered most. The long-standing county, borough, township and parochial boundaries stood firm, in spite of considerable reallocation and reformation, many areas yet enjoy the frontiers of yesteryear. This pattern, supported by the innate conservatism and solemn pride of local government, is hard to alter. Amalgamation of local governments rouses fiery and emotional feelings. Even the merging of particular services is by no means easy, and any attempts to combine police forces have always proved an arduous exercise.

The character and structure of social administration had, by and large, been set by the beginning of this century. The old poor law had combined residential treatment with the disbursement of doles. The new poor law, despite its own frigid objections, was forced to continue outdoor relief, alongside the workhouse system. The welfare state now employs both mechanisms to succour its unfortunates. There are institutions, such as orphanages and geriatric units, and there are 'outdoor' benefits for unemployment, sickness, old age and so on. In the field of public health, 'public' became the operative word, and, with a state-run health service, the triumph of municipal and national enterprise over private enterprise in the sphere of water supply, sanitation and health generally was complete.

Sometimes the continuity of Victorian institutions has apparent disadvantages. Given the go-ahead to local initiative on water supply, there has been constant bickering between areas providing and areas receiving the water. In retrospect, one might argue that a national undertaking would have been preferable, but, given the impetus of a start, it is difficult to backtrack and start again. Police areas constitute a comparable illustration. In 1856 the police force of the United Kingdom was divided into counties, with boroughs, some large, some small, dotted hither and thither. Despite pleas for a national brigade, this format is exactly the same today. The tune changes but the melody lingers on.

All these varying agencies were to be armed with expertise, and today Great Britain has an enormous army of civil and local government servants. Chadwick and his *confrères* shared the view that paid public officers were the key to efficient administrative functioning, at both national and local levels. They were opposed to the amateur bungling, the subcontracting and the hiring of help to which they were accustomed. At first expertise was not particularly effective, but with the coming of prescribed qualifications and recognised training, the picture changed radically. It is now quite commonplace for public bodies to employ not only clerical and executive personnel but all manner of specialists, such as doctors, engineers, surveyors, forensic scientists and a hundred others. The Benthamites are, in part, answerable for the proliferation, be it good or bad, of the public services.

Many commentators have called attention to the growth of bureaucracy, involving the practice of sublegislative and extra-judicial administration—for example, a nationalised board making its own regulations or haling citizens before its own tribunal. This has been seen as a threat to the rule of law and the sovereignty of parliament, those twin bastions of the British constitution. Although the Benthamites insisted that any legislation they supported was to secure rather than to infringe liberty, it must be admitted that the Chadwickians rather presumed to know what was best for people. This authoritarian tinge in Benthamism has doubtless contributed to the evolution of what has been called the 'new despotism'. Chadwick certainly put his trust not in princes nor in politicians, but rather in administrators.

In these several ways, therefore, Victorian social reform was to leave its imprint on our own century. The mood and extent of social engineering has considerably altered; this was an automatic response geared to a changing code and standard of life. It would be ludicrous to imagine the present half million unemployed and their families segregated in different wards of a workhouse, and break-fasting off a half-pint of porridge and six ounces of bread. But the mechanics of social administration appear, on inspection, to have retained much of their Victorian, and even earlier, character. That hoary old historical ham, the character transported hither from his own epoch, would obviously be startled by the changes. He might well be least surprised by the borough P.C., the social security officer and the sanitary inspector (**29, 30**).

Part Four

DOCUMENTS

The richest vein to be tapped in a study of Victorian social administration is the inexhaustible supply of documents. Whereas
there are limitations to a bibliography, the problem with the documentary evidence is where to stop, for the voluminous records of the
conscientious Victorian official are a joy to the researcher. The import of social reform is its effect on the man in the street, and the
generalised standard work, obviously, can rarely assess this impact
for an especial locality. This deficiency is well compensated for by
the wealth of local material, for, with the health, poor law and
police services operating on a local basis, many of their archives are
readily available anywhere in the country. As the Poor Law
Unions were abolished in 1929, their minute-books and so on tend

to be collected in the county and city record offices. Health and legal papers (especially on the judicial and prison side) are also to be found there, but, as the public health agencies and police forces have frequently had an unbroken administrative run since their Victorian origins, their records are normally available in the relevant libraries and town halls. Although many archives were required on active service as salvage during the last war, local governments' traditional care in husbanding its records make it one of the easiest of research topics.

At a national level, the Public Record Office has vast collections, particularly of public health and poor law correspondence and of criminal and convict returns. During the last century dozens of committees and commissions meditated these various problems and hundreds of reports were issued and thousands of returns completed. All these are available as Parliamentary Papers, and these are usually available in the larger libraries, sometimes on microcard. It is worth noting that most record offices and sizcable public libraries will undertake photocopying orders.

The following documents offer brief examples of local and national records. It cannot be urged too strongly that an anthology of documents can do no more than whet the students' appetite to seek out the full or a similar version.

POPULATION

REGISTRAR-GENERAL FIRST ANNUAL REPORT

The first annual report resulting from the Acts which established the registration of births, deaths and marriages was published in 1839 and was signed by T. H. Lister, the first Registrar-General. These yearly digests, beginning conveniently at the beginning of Victoria's reign, provide detailed statistical evidence for the researcher. This excerpt is from the introduction, and gives some idea of the scope of the enterprise. As it suggests, abstracts are given area by area, and it is possible for the local historian to paint a very full picture of population change over the years in any particular area. Causes of death are dealt with, and the impact of such information on insurance is referred to. Registration was operated by the Poor Law Commission through its Unions, and this major breakthrough in statistical collation was to be the foundation of the highly organised and controlled administrative complex in which we now live.

In the abstract of deaths (the registration of which even for this first year has been effected with signal success) I have entered into more minute details exhibiting enumerations of the deaths of persons of each sex at each successive years of age. Such details are of acknowledged value, as data for determining the laws of mortality—as bases for calculation materially affecting the interests of millions. Tables exhibiting the proportion of deaths at every successive year of age are among the most important materials from which are deduced the true principles on which should be founded the systems of Life Annuities and of Life Assurance, and the rules of Friendly Societies established for the use of the poorer classes. . . . In pursuance of these objects, I have felt that it was of great importance not only to give an abstract for the whole kingdom of England and Wales, but to exhibit the difference which prevails in different portions of the kingdom, to compare town with country— agricultural districts with manufacturing and mining districts —the hilly with the low and level—the maritime with the inland—the eastern and northern with the western and southern parts. Nor are these diversities matters of merely curious speculation, but may be made the source of important benefits, especially to the poorer classes. . . .

I will now offer a few observations upon the degree of success which has attended Registration in the first year under the new system, in regard to the number of Births, Deaths and Marriages registered, in England and Wales, as appears from the certified copies deposited in this office. Those numbers have been as follows:

Births	399,712
Deaths	335,956
Marriages	111,481

Parliamentary Papers 1839 (187) XVI. 1

REPORT ON INTERMENT BY EDWIN CHADWICK

Mr Leonard's fearful testimony was duplicated by many others up and down the country. It underlines the impact of 'congregation' in no uncertain manner, and draws attention to the perils of disease and poverty in such surroundings. Overcrowding, so poignantly illustrated by the lodging-houses, was the crucial element in the Victorian social milieu, and, with a sad irony, it is the Report on Interment which provides the most vivid and harrowing picture.

26.   Mr Leonard, surgeon and medical officer of the parish of St Martin's-in-the-Fields, gives the following instances of the circumstances in which the poorest class of inhabitants die, which may be adduced as exemplifications of the dreadful state of circumstances in which the survivors are placed for the want of adequate accommodation for the remains immediately after death, and previous to the interment:—

There are some houses in my district that have from 45 to 60 persons of all ages under one roof, and in the event of death, the body often occupies the only bed till they raise money to pay for a coffin, which is often several days. . . . Of course the tenants are never free from fevers and diarrhoea and the mortality is great. The last class live, for the most part, in lodging houses, where shelter is obtained, with a bed of straw, for 2d to 4d per night, and where this is not obtainable, the arches under the Adelphi afford a shelter. In the lodging-rooms I have seen the beds placed so close together as not to allow room to pass between them, and occupied by both sexes indiscriminately. I have known six people sleep in a room about nine feet square, with only one small window, about 17 inches by 12 inches; and there are some sleeping rooms in this district in which you cannot scarcely see your hand at noonday.

How long is the dead body retained in the room beside the living?—If the person has subscribed to a club, or the friends are in circumstances to afford the expense of the funeral, it takes place, generally, on the following Sunday, if the death has occurred earlier in the week; but if towards the end of the week, then it is sometimes postponed till the Sunday week

73

after, if the weather permit; in one case it was twelve days. . . .
In what condition is the corpse usually, or frequently, retained?—Amongst the Irish, it does not signify of what disease
the person may have died, it is retained often for many days,
laid out upon the only bed, perhaps. . . . Thus fevers and
other contagious diseases are fearfully propagated . . . and this
spring I removed a girl, named Wilson, to the infirmary of the
Workhouse, from a room in the same court. I could not remain
two minutes in it; the horrible stench arose from a corpse
which had died of phthisis twelve days before, and the coffin
stood across the foot of the bed, within eighteen inches of it.
This was a small room not above ten feet by twelve feet square,
and a fire always in it, being (as in most cases of a like kind) the
only one for sleeping, living and cooking in.

Parliamentary Papers 1843 XII

JEREMY BENTHAM AND INDIVIDUALISM

Here one has a denunciation of the needless restrictions imposed on individuals, and, by implication, a cry for laissez-faire in J. Bentham, Truth against Ashurst, *(1823) p. 234. The Utilitarian yardstick, as applied to legislation, made a strong appeal to the nineteenth century radical, as, indeed, it does to many today, and the polemical style of this extract recalls that laissez-faire was not 'easy acquiescence' but 'a war-cry'.*

Truth.—I sow corn: partridges eat it, and if I attempt to defend it against the partridge, I am fined or sent to gaol: all this, for fear a great man, who is above sowing corn, should be in want of partridges.

The trade I was born to is overstocked: hands are wanting in another. If I offer to work at that other, I may be sent to gaol for it. Why? Because I have not been working at it as an apprentice for seven years. What's the consequence? That, as there is no work for me in my original trade, I must either come upon this parish or starve.

There is no employment for me in my own parish: there is abundance in the next. Yet if I offer to go there, I am driven away. Why? Because I might become unable to work one of these days, and so I must not work while I am able. I am thrown upon one parish now, for fear I should fall upon another, forty or fifty years hence. At this rate how is work ever to get done? If a man is not poor, he won't work: and if he is poor, the laws won't let him. How then is it that so much is done as is done? As pockets are picked—by stealth, and because the law is so wicked that it is only here and there that a man can be found wicked enough to think of executing it.

Pray, Mr Justice, how is the community you speak of the better for any of these restraints? and where is the necessity of them? and how is safety strengthened or good order benefited by them?

document 4

THE ANDOVER WORKHOUSE SCANDAL

REPORT FROM THE SELECT COMMITTEE ON THE ANDOVER UNION

The Andover Scandal of 1845–46 highlighted the hardship of the work-house regime. McDougal, the master of the Andover workhouse, had a reputation for gross inhumanity, and rumours of excess cruelty eventually led to a public enquiry. Bone crushing was a normal mode of pauper work—the bones of horses, dogs and other animals, including, it was hinted some from local graveyards, were crushed for fertilizer for the nearby farms. So hungry were the paupers that they scrambled for these rotting bones, and bone-crushing became the centrepiece of a case followed eagerly by the public and extensively covered by The Times. *The enquiry had all kinds of political repercussions. Chadwick emerged especially well, and reached at this time the height of his prestige and power. Andover was but the most notorious example of workhouse cruelty. There were several other major scandals and incidents galore, all faithfully recorded in the press.*

Evidence of Charles Lewis, labourer.

9828　(Mr Wakley) What work were you employed about when you were in the workhouse?—I was employed breaking bones.

9829　Were other men engaged in the same work?—Yes.

9830　Was that the only employment you had?—That was the only employment I had at the time I was there.

9831　Was the smell very bad?—Very bad.

9832　Did it appear to affect your health?—It did a great deal mine, and appeared to affect the others.

9833　How many men were so employed?—Whether it was nine or ten boxes round the room, I don't recollect.

9834　Was it a close room or shed?—It was a very close room.

9835　How did you break them?—We had a large iron bar to break them with.

9836　Something like a rammer?—Yes.

9837　Had you no other employment at all?—No, not while I was there, but breaking the bones.

9838　What sort of bones did they appear to be?—All sorts.

9839　During the time you were so employed, did you ever see any of the men gnaw anything or eat anything from those bones?—I have seen them eat marrow out of the bones.

9840 You were not examined before Mr Parker, the Assistant Commissioner?—No.

9841 Have you often seen them eat the marrow?—I have.

9842 Did they state why they did it?—I really believe they were very hungry.

9843 Did you yourself feel extremely hungry at that time?—I did, but my stomach would not take it.

9844 You could not swallow the marrow?—No.

9845 Did you see any of the men gnaw the meat from the bones?—Yes.

9846 Did they use to steal the bones and hide them away?—Yes.

9847 Have you seen them have a scramble and quarrel amongst the bones?—I do not know that I have seen them scramble, but I have seen them hide them.

9848 And when a fresh set of bones came in, did they keep a sharp look-out for the best?—Yes.

9849 Was that a regular thing?—While I was there.

Parliamentary Papers 1846 V

document 5

THE POOR LAW BOARD AND CLITHEROE UNION

POOR LAW BOARD: CORRESPONDENCE WITH CLITHEROE POOR LAW UNION, 1850

The Public Record Office has voluminous log-books of the correspondence between unions and the Poor Law Commission and Board. Huge foolscap volumes have the letters received pasted in, together with a laboriously written copy of the answer. This letter is one such included in this crude filing system. It relates a sad but typical story, and it also indicates the puny powers allowed the central body at this time. The secretary of the board had scribbled across the letter the following instruction to his clerk: 'State that the board have no power to order relief, but will make enquiry of guardians as to his case'.

Gentlemen of Honour and Commissioners of the Poor Law at Somerset House, London. I beg permission to lay a case before you of one name of Wm. Martin hawker by occupation; which has a wife and five children . . . who is reduced by five months sickness of his wife. The surgeon stated that she was in danger of losing her eyesight if she did not be cautious. She asked him if moving to the seashore would be of any means, he replied he thought it would, so I appeared at the Board of Guardians the Tuesday following and I asked them if they would be so kind as to grant me a trifle of money to take her to the seashore. They asked me if I had got a certificate from the surgeon, I answered no sir, they answered if I had brought one they said they could have done better with me if I had brought one, so I prolonged the time another week, and I got a certificate from Mr Patchett the surgeon. So I appeared again at the Board, on the Tuesday following but they would not grant me a penny so I was resolved before she should lose her eyesight I would sell all my chattles so on Sunday following I contrived for her to go down to Blackpool, and she remained there a few days, and returned home again much the better. And in a few days afterwards she was struck with the Cholera . . . and so I passed on to the thirteenth day of December 1849 she went to the Relieving Officer and he gave her an order for the workhouse and she asked him for a horse and cart for it is twelve miles from my cottage and I am sure my children cannot walk such a distance but he answered he would not . . . so my brother got a horse and cart and took me and the family to the workhouse and we stayed there till the fifteenth of January 1850, and then I appeared at the Board again and asked them if they would be so kind as to allow me to depart from the workhouse and allow my family to abide in the workhouse and I would try to gain a few goods but they would not . . . the governor came to me as I was weaving and said well martin, you must weave five cuts every week each cut was forty yards in length. I answered I cannot so he answered I must weave them or flit then he went to Mrs Martin and said well Mrs Martin you must weave three cuts of the same kind every week so she began to weep for she could not do it, for she had five children to look after. . . . Gentlemen—is this not an unreasonable request so on the twentieth I left there so if it would please your honours to look into my present state for I cannot bear it. . . . Yours respectfully, Wm. Martin.

P.R.O.M.H. 12/5754.

document 6

UNION BUSINESS

MINUTES OF WEST DERBY BOARD OF GUARDIANS, 17 JAN. 1877

This endpiece to a standard guardians' monthly meeting demonstrates the variety of union business, and many meetings ended with such a flurry of resolutions. Officials are appointed, at depressingly low salaries, and health matters, such as smallpox and the deaf and dumb, fall within the guardians' ken. The combining of apprenticeship and school boards seems a mixture of ancient and modern. By an act of 1876 unions were permitted to organise school attendance committees, in order to encourage the use and growth of schools, and were also allowed to reimburse fees for impoverished parents.

Resolved that Peter Anderson be appointed assistant lunatic attendant at Walton workhouse with a salary of £30 per annum.

Resolved that Matilda Lunt be appointed probationary nurse at Walton workhouse with a salary of £14 per annum.

Resolved that Mr Fitzpatrick be written to respecting the case of Martha Appleton of Blackhorse Lane, who had made application to him for medical assistance in a case of small pox and who was referred to Mr Parry for assistance and was charged 2/6d.

Resolved that Elizabeth Gartland of 12 Brunswick Terrace, Kirkdale, be admitted to the deaf and dumb institution at the cost of this union and also that Samuel Munnerly of Knotty Ash be admitted. . . .

Resolved that the several relieving officers be requested to assist the school boards throughout the union in the investigation of application by persons residing in their respective district for school fees. . . .

Resolved that John Burnett a poor boy chargeable to this union be apprenticed for 5 years to George Richardson of 99 Farnworth St., West Derby, tailor. That a premium of £4 be paid with such apprentice by annual instalments of one pound and that the apprentice be allowed 2 suits of clothes.

Resolved that the clerk do report the number of removal cases in the workhouse with the names and date of entrance.

L. W. Heintz.
Chairman.

PUBLIC HEALTH: LOCAL INITIATIVE

General Board of Health—Correspondence with the Ormskirk Local Board of Health

The hefty correspondence of the General Board of Health is to be found in the Public Record Office, and, as with the poor law files, a considerable amount of flesh may be found to fill out the skeletal nature of local minute-books. This letter, for example, answers a question which every board prompts—given the need for local initiative, who stimulates it? In this case it was the assiduous W. L. Welsby, who, well known as an Ormskirk guardian, practically began this new venture all but single-handed. It is interesting to observe that the worry of 'Irish lodging houses', even in a small market-town, was crucial. Mr Welsby was chairman of the union 'sanatory committee', yet another illustration of the ubiquitous activity of the poor law agencies. Ormskirk, incidentally, was one of the very first boards to complete satisfactory watering and sewering schemes, under the direction of the notable Victorian engineer and protégé of Chadwick, Robert Rawlinson.

Sir,

I am obliged for your attention to my letter and now beg to forward petition praying for the adoption of the Health of Towns Act from the inhabitants of Ormskirk signed by 164. The number of rated inhabitants by the last rate book is upwards of 1100 so that it will be perceived that it is signed by a number exceeding the required amount. There appears to be a very favourable feeling towards its adoption generally and many more signatures might have been obtained but it was thought unnecessary. I shall feel greatly obliged by its presentation. I have deferred forwarding the petition in the hope that the enforcement of the epidemic disease act and the order of the commissioners might have answered our purpose but perceiving that there is no apparent available power of dealing summarily with Irish lodging houses which have become from our proximity to Liverpool quite a pest to the town it will avail little as a permanent remedy. The town wants sewering too and an ample supply of water without which no efficient sanatory measures can be carried out. The attendance of an officer as early as practicable is earnestly requested; in the meantime I will as Chairman of the sanatory committee under the directions of the guardians work out the order of the commissioners as far as practicable. I shall be glad to give all publicity to the intentions of the officer's attendance to make the necessary enquiry and shall be glad of any information to enable me to assist him in his enquiries. Perhaps you will intimate whether the surveying officer will make the necessary enquiry for himself or he will expect the inhabitants to be prepared with evidence for his consideration.

I am, Sir,

Yours most obediently,
W. L. Welsby.

P.R.O.M.H. 13/138.

REPORT OF THE GENERAL BOARD OF HEALTH
ON CHOLERA

This extract clearly defines the prevailing 'atmospheric' and 'non-contagious' view of disease. It maintains the preventive theme firmly, and the link between public health and the poor law is well indicated. A less obvious link, between public health and police, is also suggested. The medical remedies seem odd today, and they lie uneasily side by side with the stark realism of the practical steps taken. Many Victorian towns were hit by cholera, and records of local 'lay committees' and emergency fever hospitals are frequently available. Sometimes there was a crisis of confidence between doctors and public, with doctors accused of experiments on the bodies of hospitalised patients, and occasional riots occurred.

Although it is so far true that certain conditions may favour its spread from person to person, as when great numbers of sick are crowded together in close unventilated apartments, yet this is not to be considered as affecting the general principle of its non-contagious nature; nor are such conditions likely to occur in this country; moreover the preventive measures founded on the theory of contagion, namely, internal quarantine regulations, sanitary cordons, and the isolation of the sick . . . have been recently abandoned in all countries where Cholera has appeared, from the general experience of their inefficiency. . . .

The chief predisposing causes of every epidemic, and especially of Cholera, are damp, moisture, filth, animal and vegetable matters in a state of decomposition, and, in general, whatever produces atmospheric impurity; all of which have the effect of lowering the health and vigour of the system, and of increasing the susceptibility to disease particularly among the young, the aged and the feeble.

The attacks of Cholera are uniformly found to be most frequent and virulent in low lying districts, on the banks of rivers, in the neighbourhood of sewer mouths, and wherever there are large collections of refuse, particularly amidst human dwellings. . . . Householders of all classes should be warned, that their first means of safety lies in the removal of dung-heaps and solid and liquid filth of every description from beneath or about their houses and premises. . . .

The Union Medical Officers, whose duties take them to the relief of the destitute sick, are necessarily familiar with the places in which the disease is most prevalent and fatal, and these are invariably found to be the dirtiest localities, where, consequently, the cleansing operations are most required; and the Nuisances Removal Act imposes upon the Guardians the duty of directing and enforcing the proper performance of these operations.

In several districts the police, in going their usual rounds, have been employed with great advantage in reporting daily as to the houses, courts, alleys, passages and streets within their district most in need of cleansing, as to the carelessness or neglect of the scavengers in the performance of their duties, and as to the existence of nuisances of various kinds. . . .

Highly important services have been rendered by the parochial clergy and other ministers of religion, in association with lay committees, for the purpose of maintaining a system of house-to-house visitation in the more depressed districts. . . .

Medical authorities are agreed . . . that the most simple will suffice . . . and that the following . . . may be regarded as among the most useful; namely, 20 grains of opiate confection mixed with 2 tablespoonfuls of peppermint-water, or with a little weak brandy and water repeated every three or four hours, or oftener, if the attack is severe, until the looseness of the bowels is stopped; or an ounce of chalk mixture, with 10 or 15 grains of the aromatic confection, and from 5 to 10 drops of laudanum, repeated in the same manner. . . .

Parliamentary Papers 1849 XXIV

PUBLIC HEALTH: LOCAL SURVEY

MINUTES OF GARSTON LOCAL BOARD OF HEALTH 1854-55

Volumes of minutes of local boards of health are available in small towns as well as large, and the routine operations of a local board may be traced here. They often spell out tales of hesitant planning and indecisive action, with surveyors and engineers being asked to do too much work too quickly in a new and relatively unknown field. The above extracts show how difficult it was to obtain a survey of a small area, let alone to begin draining or sewering it. The problem of suddenly imposing comprehensive underground systems on overcrowded streets of houses was, of course, a daunting one.

5 Sept. 1854. Resolved on the motion of Mr Morris, seconded by Mrs Moss, that the works and health committee be authorised to advertise for tenders for a plan and report of the district according to the regulations of the General Board of Health.

7 Nov. 1854. Resolved unanimously that the tender of Mr Edward Gotto to make a survey and plans of the district for £90 be accepted.

5 Dec. 1854. Resolved on the motion of Mr Watts, seconded by Mr Lightbody, that Mr Gotto be informed that the detailed plans must be on mounted paper.

10 April 1855. The chairman called the attention of the board that the time when Mr Gotto according to his contract was to have finished the plans of the district expired on the 1st instant.

1 May 1855. Resolved . . . that the board is desirous of having the survey and plans and requesting him to fix the time when the board might expect to receive the plans.

5 June 1855. Ordered that the law clerk write and express the great dissatisfaction of the board at the delay in the delivery of the plans and urge dispatch.

4 Sept. 1855. Mr Gotto's letters of the 1st and 3rd September being read, the latter suggesting that a special meeting of the board should be held to receive the plans.

11 Sept. 1855. Mr Gotto having attended with the plans of the district, resolved on the motion of Mr Cooper, seconded by Mr Goodwin, that the plans be referred to the Works and Health Committee.

6 Nov. 1855. The letter of General Board dated 24th October 1855 stating the approval of Mr Gotto's plans was read.

Mr Gotto's letter of 31st October and his account for the balance due to him for the survey and plans being read, ordered that same be referred to the Finance Committee.

LAW AND ORDER

The Constabulary Commission, 1836–39

Apart from the published annals of the Constabulary Commission, the Public Record Office holds several batches of miscellaneous papers, memoranda and evidence presented to that commission. This is an extract from one of dozens of questionnaires completed, under the guidance of prison governors, by convicts. The questions, although answered with a predictable rigidity, offer an approximate sociological survey of Victorian crime. Later questions were much more loaded, in terms of building the case for preventive policing, but these initial fifteen questions are of value. Despite John Edwards's broken home, his upbringing was relatively solid educationally and religiously; in brief, the ease or greater 'eligibility' of crime was, according to Chadwick's evaluation, the temptation.

1. What is your name, age, and the offence for which you are in prison?
John Edwards 15 years of age, for taking a drawer containing money out of a shop.
2. Are you single, married, or a widower? Have you children—how many?
Single.
3. What has been your calling, or occupation?
I have been two years in the employ of a Copper Plate Printer and 6 months in a Druggist Shop.
4. Are your Parents living? If not, what was your age when they or either of them died?
Both living.
5. If either Father or Mother be dead, has the survivor married again? If so, how long ago?
Both living.
6. Are you illegitimate? or a foundling?
Not illegitimate.
7. Where were you brought up? At the house of your Parents or at that of any other relation or friend? or in the work-house, or in the streets, being left without care and control?
At the house of my parents.

8. Of what calling were your Parents? Did they, or either of them, continue long in any service?

My father an auctioneer and apprazier in business for himself.

9. Of what character was your Father? Was he honest, industrious, and sober?

Honest, industrious and sober.

10. Of what character was your Mother? Was she honest, virtuous, industrious, and sober?

My mother left my father about two years ago and lives with another man.

11. Did your Parents regularly attend a place of worship, and require you to accompany them?

My father regularly attended a place of worship and required me to accompany him.

12. What care was taken of you by your Parents? Did you ever run away from them? What induced you to do so? Were you punished for doing so; and in what way?

Great care was taken of me by my parents. I have run away from them induced to do so by other boys. I have been punished for doing so by my father by fastening me to the bedpost and flogging me with a rope.

13. Did the occupation of either of your Parents necessarily take them much from home?

My father's business took him from home in the day time, my mother never from house.

14. Did you attend any school? If so, for how long, and at what description of school; whether Dame School, National School, British and Foreign School, Sunday School, Church School, or Dissenting School?

I went to school for about 10 years for which schooling my father paid for.

15. Were you taught to read and write?
Both.

P.R.O.H.O. 73/2 Pt. I.

RETURN OF CONVICTS CONFINED IN
PORTLAND PRISON, 1849

The Public Record Office includes quarterly returns of the convict hulks and prisons, from which it is possible to build up some picture of the incidence of Victorian crime and the harsh punishment meted out. The prevalence of crimes of gain is evident in this abridged sample, as is also the odd logic of the sentencing—twenty years, for example, for setting fire to straw. A point of interest is the geographical spread of the convictions, indicative of the trend towards the national gaol and away from the county prison and parish lock-up. Pre. Con. or P.C. means previous conviction, indict. means indictment and C.C.Court means Central Criminal Court, London.

NAME	AGE	OFFENCE	WHERE	SENTENCE
James Hackett	21	Felony	Salford	7
John Taylor	20	Stealing a file and moneys	Leicester	7
John Brown	20	Larceny previous con.	C.C. Court	7
James Barker	47	Stealing fowls, 2 indicts.	Exeter	14
William Johnson	25	Setting fire to 2 stacks of straw	Stafford	20
James Sweeney	58	Uttering count coin P.C.	Caenarvon	15
George Williams	21	Burglary P.C.	C.C. Court	10
Francis Best	35	Housebreaking & Larceny	Worcester	15
John Henry	36	Uttering forged notes	Glasgow	20
Thomas Hartshorn	33	Robbery with violence P.C.	Liverpool	15
Samuel Laughton	22	Burglary, stealing silver spoons etc.	Nottingham	14
Thomas Robinson	23	Burglary and theft, 2 indict.	Maidstone	14
Martin Stone	22	House stealing	Dorchester	15
Richard Ashford	58	Stealing 3 lbs of pork P.C.	Exeter	10
John Dobson	28	Stealing money from the person P.C.	Stafford	14
Samuel Diggle	36	Burglary	Liverpool	15
George Goult	22	Robbery P.C.	Chelmsford	12

Robert Holder	23	Stealing from a dwelling £15 & pr pistols	Portsmouth	15
Richard Jones	36	Warehouse breaking & stealing malt & hops	Reading	15
Hugh King alias Cameron	36	Theft by housebreaking	Glasgow	14
Austin Montroe	34	Larceny in a dwelling to the value of £5 P.C.	C.C. Court	15

P.R.O.H.O. 8/102.

COUNTY CONSTABULARIES

Home Office—Correspondence with the County Constabularies, 1839

This short extract is culled from the foolscap books of the Home Office in which the clerks copied out the letters and titles of enclosure despatched on constabulary business. It is a random page from the earliest year of the Rural Constabulary Act, when county forces were first being formed. Its brevity is representative of the rather frail link between Home Office and counties—the gap in dates between letters suggest a sparse correspondence. Typically enough, most of the points raised here are legal technicalities about 'local difficulties' or the position of watchmen. They were transmitted to the 'L.O.' (law office) for a definitive opinion. Lord Normanby was Home Secretary at this time, and S. M. Phillipps a civil servant of high repute.

G. Maule Esquire.   Whitehall 4th Nov. 1839.
Enclosing copy of instructions to County Constables, and requesting the opinion of the L.O. whether they may be issued.   S.M.

The Solicitors of the Treasury.   Whitehall 13th Nov. 1839.
Enclosing copy of letter from inspector of police, Wrexham and requesting the opinion of the L.O. whether the Act 3 & 4 Wm. 4 C. 90 for appointing and paying watchman etc. is repealed by the 2 & 3 Vict. C. 93.   S.M.P.

The Solicitors to the Treasury.   Whitehall 13th Nov. 1839.
Sir,
I am directed by the Marquis of Normanby to transmit to you the enclosed letter from Wm. Kenyon, Chairman of the Shropshire Quarter Sessions, on the subject of local difficulties which appear to have arisen in carrying the Rural Police Act into effect. I also transmit the cases alluded to in Wm. Kenyon's letter and I am to desire you will lay the name before Att. G. & Sol. General and move them to report their opinion on all the points referred to for Lord Normanby's information.
I am etc.,
S. M. Phillipps.

P.R.O.H.O. 65/4.

WATCH COMMITTEE AT WORK

LIVERPOOL WATCH COMMITTEE MINUTES. 3 SEPT. 1853

Watch committee monthly minutes are available in some towns as far back as 1835, and they provide chapter and verse of police development. The watch committee managed the finances and manning of the force, which, it will be noted, also handled fires. The provincial reliance on Metropolitan police guidance is hinted at, and there are also three sound illustrations of the dangers of police-work—from being hurt on duty, from false accusation (at a time when the police were often in bad public odour) and even from superior officers. The police were also used to seek out nuisance, as the odd spectacle of a dangerous quarry in a city street exemplifies.

Resolved that the several bills as detailed in the abstract book of this date folio 187 amounting to £42.17.8 be referred to the Finance Committee for payment.

The Head Constable certified that the wages for the police Force for the week ended on Monday last amounted as per wages book in North and South Divisions to £560.9.7 and in the Dock Division to £298.0.9. Resolved upon the report of the surgeon and head constable that the wages of those constables who have been hurt on duty duly amounting to £16.2.1 be allowed and paid.

A memorial from police constable 755 John Wood (suspended by the head constable for alleged violence to a prisoner) praying to be reinstated—also a memorial from police constable 657 George Neilson (also suspended for the same alleged cause) praying to be reinstated were read, and the officers having appealed to the character of the person in whose charge their suspension had taken place, and their own characters as appearing in the Report Books of the head constable it appeared their own characters were satisfactory and that the character of Thomas Eaves, the person charging them was as follows:

He had been fifteen times convicted for assault and other offences. . . .

Resolved, on the recommendation of the head constable that they be reinstated.

The head constable having reported on the dangerous condition of a quarry in Hygenia Street belonging to Mr Peacock resolved that the town clerk be instructed to write to Mr Peacock requiring him to render such quarry safe to the public. . . .

The head constable presented a report to this committee on the subject of his inspection of the Metropolitan police force. . . .

The following resolution from the Hackney Carriage Committee of the 30th August 1853 was read: The committee having investigated the charge preferred against Inspector Johnson for interfering with P.C. 493 West and it appearing that Inspector Johnson had improperly interfered with West resolved that Inspector Johnson be admonished by the chairman and he was called in and admonished accordingly. . . .

The head constable submitted the fire police book containing reports of fires which had taken place during the last week.

J. A. Tobin

(Chairman)

SYDNEY WEBB AND COLLECTIVISM

Webb was a characteristic and vigorous figure in the establishment of the collectivist state, and this wry passage illustrates the creeping, almost unnoticed, spread of state intervention and its organic growth from Benthamite principles of self-help.

The practical man, oblivious or contemptuous of any theory of the social organism or general principles of social organisation, has been forced, by the necessities of the time, into an ever-deepening collectivist channel. Socialism, of course, he still rejects and despises. The individualist town councillor will walk along the municipal pavement, lit by municipal gas, and cleansed by municipal brooms with municipal water, and seeing, by the municipal clock in the municipal market, that he is too early to meet his children coming from the municipal school, hard by the county lunatic asylum and municipal hospital, will use the national telegraph system to tell them not to walk through the municipal park, but to come by the municipal tramway, to meet him in the municipal reading-room, by the municipal art gallery, museum, and library, where he intends to consult some of the national publications in order to prepare his next speech in the municipal town hall, in favour of the nationalisation of canals and the increase of Government control over the railway system. 'Socialism, Sir,' he will say, 'don't waste the time of a practical man by your fantastic absurdities. Self-help, Sir, individual self-help, that's what's made our city what it is'.

From Sydney Webb, *Socalism in England* (1890) pp. 116–7.

POVERTY NEAR THE END OF THE CENTURY

MINUTES OF TOXTETH PARK BOARD OF GUARDIANS, 2 MARCH 1899

This straightforward record of a Guardians' meeting is similar to thousands held between 1834 and 1929, and now available to the student in huge foolscap volumes of manuscript. In a sense its main value is its similarity to **doc. 6,** *indicating the uniformity of poor law administration over the decades. Finance and management were still the chief concerns, with formal confirmation of accounts and orders completed without difficulty. One or two points are of interest. The appearance of four women on a fairly strong committee is a definite sign of the times, and it is sometimes forgotten that women busied themselves with such local matters well before obtaining the franchise. The mention of school fees is another pointer. The Guardians undertook certain educational duties in the years after the 1870 Education Act. This was the kind of 'outdoor relief' Chadwick abhorred, but he would have welcomed the new view of settlement suggested by the case of Charles Crompton, the strict ruling with regard to visitors, and the growing health work done by the union.*

At a meeting of the Guardians held on the 2nd March 1899; present, Mr Killip in the chair, Miss Booth, Mrs Ellis, Miss Bowring, Mrs Healey, Rev. I. P. Baynes, Rev. L. Harris, Messrs. Abercrombie, Paull, Gastting, Thomas, Titley, Turner, Skinner, Edwards, Mather.

Minutes of the last meeting read and signed.

The balance in the hands of the treasurer £478.9s.6d. . . .

The application and report books of the relieving officers, the relief order books and school fees books (duly written up) were laid before the Guardians.

Submitted estimates of provisions and other articles required in the workhouse during the ensuing week and also for the home, Richmond Lodge. Orders for which were directed to be issued. . . .

Charles Crompton—a lunatic. Resolved that Charles Crompton, a pauper lunatic, in the Whittingham asylum and thither from the Bolton Union be admitted to be settled within this township and that the cost of his maintenance therein be paid by this township. . . .

Mr Cole—right to visit workhouse. Read letter dated 27th ulto. from the Rev. W. G. Cole on the subject of his right to administer religious assistance to the inmates of the workhouse. Resolved that the clerk reply that the Guardians do not wish to continue the controversy and that a clergymans' rights will be: 1. that he will be allowed to visit any inmates on the same terms and conditions as other visitors.

2. that he will be allowed to visit and afford religious assistance to any inmate who may desire it.

Tuberculosis—joint committee. Resolved that the chairman, vice-chairman, and the clerk be the representatives of this township on the joint committee to carry out the scheme decided upon at the conference of the 3 Liverpool Boards of Guardians held on the 22nd ulto., namely to make separate provision for 25 beds for the treatment of tuberculosis. . . .

Latrines etc.—old male hospital. Resolved that the tender of Mr Isaac Dilworth of Wavertree for building boundary wall, latrines etc. at the old male hospital for the sum of £264 be accepted. . . .

PUBLIC HEALTH—AND WASTE

LITTLE WOOLTON LOCAL BOARD MINUTES, 6 JULY 1885

*Boards of Health met on a monthly or, as in this case, a weekly basis.
There were usually twelve members, but attendance, as here, was often
six or seven. They had extensive powers, and, for example, their
authority over building planning sounds rather a modern note. They
also had considerable financial powers for levying general and special
rates of a comparatively high nature. Perhaps the abiding illustration
here is the small and perhaps wasteful nature of the units involved.
The earnest consideration of steam-rollers, Mrs French's drain and two
deaths are as typical of the over-solemn character of Victorian local
government as of its too frequently tiny ambit.*

Present—Mr John Busby in the chair; Mr G. H. Robertson,
Mr Elkanah Healey, Mr Thomas Dobell, Mr Harold Cunning-
ham, Mr Harry Jump, Mr Sam Sanday. . . .

By the Collector's collecting and deposit account for the past
month it appeared that he had collected the following sums
on the undermentioned account viz.

General District Rate	£20	9	6
Highway Rate	£27	7	4
	£47	16	10

Ordered that the collectors' A/C in the ledger be debitted and
the foregoing accounts credited with the separate amounts. . . .
Hire of steam roller—read a letter from the clerk to the West
Derby local board stating that the board was willing to hire
its steam roller to other local boards at a charge of two guineas
per day. The surveyor reported that the Widnes local board
hired out its steam roller for the use of other local boards at a
charge of £1 10s. od. per day. Resolved that the surveyor be
requested to ascertain from the Widnes local board whether
a charge was made for the time occupied by the steam roller in
travelling to and from the place where it was required and
when the same would be available for hire to his board and
report to the next meeting.

Drain under Mrs French's houses: Read a letter from the medical officer of health dated the 19th June 1885 stating that he had inspected the drain running under Mrs French's houses in Halewood Road and that he had found that the water contained sewage. . . .

Medical officer's Report: The law clerk read the report of the medical officer of health for the past quarter as follows: 'there have been but 2 deaths registered as having occurred in the township during the past quarter; both cases persons over 60 years of age. Eight births have also been registered during the quarter. A few isolated cases of scarlatina and measles, occurring principally amongst children have come under my notice. . . . The board may be congratulated on the unusually healthy condition of the township. . . .

Building Plans: Plans were submitted by Mr Sherlock, architect, for alterations to Mr Gladstone's shippon in Vale Road. Resolved that the same be approved of subject to the work being carried out to the satisfaction of the board's surveyor.

document 17

SANITATION, DEATHS AND DISEASE

REPORT OF THE MEDICAL OFFICER OF HEATH, 1893; PRESENTED
TO CHESHIRE COUNTY COUNCIL PUBLIC HEALTH COMMITTEE

*On the formation of county councils in 1888, a county medical officer
was appointed whose duties included the publication of an annual report.
These included both a general summary, illustrated below, and reports
on each locality. They can provide a student with a history of public
health for any township over the last eighty years. Population, deaths,
diseases, sanitation, food and drugs and so on are dealt with in detail.
This extract reveals that the state of hospitals was still far from satisfactory and that zymotic, that is epidemic, diseases were still in evidence.*

The number of Urban Sanitary Districts in the administrative
county is 34–5 municipal boroughs and 29 other urban sanitary districts. There are 11 rural sanitary districts wholly
within the administrative county, and portions of 6 other rural
sanitary districts. . . .

The great difference in the density of population in the sub-
divisions of the county has already been noted. In the various
sanitary districts it is yet more marked. Thus in Altrincham
urban district there were 19 persons to an acre, and in the
Middlewich and Runcorn urban districts 17 persons to an
acre, whilst in two urban districts, Buglawton and Tarporley,
there were more than two acres to a person. . . .

This is a matter of interest, as other things being equal the
insalubrity of a place may be expected to increase with the
density of population. . . .

Deaths—the number of deaths registered in the administrative
county was 10,333. The natural increase of the population
(excess of births over deaths) . . . was 5,823 i.e. 563 in excess of
the estimated increase for 1893. The death rate for the county
was 18.8. There is considerable difference in the death rates of
different districts. They range from 26.2 in the urban district
of Runcorn and 25 per 1000 in the borough of Stalybridge to
less than 8 per 1000 in the Cheshire portion of the Warrington
rural district, while in the Cheshire portion of Drayton there
was no death. . . .

Zymotic Diseases—The number of deaths registered in the county which were entered to one or other of the seven principal zymotic diseases was 1,370. . . .

. . . How singularly inadequate the provision is to meet the requirements of an area with a population of about 550,000 must be obvious. And the provision is even more inadequate than it looks on paper. Some are not kept in readiness when patients leave, some though in use during 1893 may have since been abandoned, pulled down or let as cottage accommodation. . . .

In 1893 there were 4,863 cases of infectious disease notified, and only 690 (14.1%) received hospital treatment of any kind. Patients are sent to Chester Infirmary, Stockport Borough Hospital, Warrington Hospital and Monsall Hospital, and several are treated at various workhouses, still many who cannot be properly housed and isolated at home are not removed, and remain as possible sources of infection to members of their families and neighbours.

CRIME IN LIVERPOOL

CITY OF LIVERPOOL: REPORT ON THE POLICE ESTABLISHMENT
AND THE STATE OF CRIME 1898

Another source of police history is the annual report made to a watch committee by its head or chief constable. In rich detail they offer statistics of crimes, licensing and drunkenness—still a major vice of the English. It is of interest to note that, whereas Saturday's drunks were predictably the most numerous, Sunday, although a holiday, had by far the fewest. The report mentions the Home Office annual inspection, a feature of police life since 1856, and the fire brigade, as yet under police supervision.

To the Chairman and members of the Watch Committee.
Gentlemen,

I have the honour to present my 18th report upon the crime of the city and upon the state of the police establishment, being that for the year ended 31st Decenmber 1898.

The figures for the year seem to afford, on the whole, a subject for congratulation, and this notwithstanding the fact that they again disclose a slight increase in the total number of indictable offences, viz 4,314 cases against 4,126 in 1897. This increase, however, consists entirely of cases of simple larceny (which numbered 203 more in 1898 than in 1897) and may be practically considered as neutralized by the decrease of 286 in the number of non-indictable offences involving dishonesty, i.e. unlawful possession etc. The most satisfactory feature in connection with the number of indictable offences is the steady and considerable decrease of offences against the person, the number of which in 1898 was only 188, against 224 in 1897, and 269 in 1896. The decrease of 36 cases last year was made up of 5 cases less of attempted murder, 2 less of manslaughter, and 29 less of wounding etc. So far from being neutralized, these figures are strengthened by the return of non-indictable offences which shows 81 fewer cases of common assault, and 766 fewer cases of drunk, drunk and riotous etc. . . . Licensing Acts—the number of licensed houses in the city has been decreased by 18 public-houses and 2 beer-houses, and increased by 5 off licenses. Allowing for these variations, the number of licensed premises now in the city is: Public-houses: 1,865; Beer-houses: 244; Off licenses: 153. Total 2,262. Their conduct has been almost uniformly good. . . . Drunkenness:—The total number of cases (4,339) has already been referred to. The number of arrests during the year was 4,292, the arrests for each day of the week being as follows:— Sunday: 294; Monday: 703; Tuesday: 544; Wednesday: 452; Thursday: 401; Friday: 501; Saturday: 1,397. . . .

Annual Inspection. The annual inspection of the force took place on the 24th and 25th May, by Sir Herbert Croft, Bart, Her Majesty's Inspector for the Northern Division of England and Wales. He also examined the books of the various departments, divisions and bridewells.

Fire Brigade Tables. Number of fires—the total number of fires attended during the year was 801 against 696 last year. . . .

J. W. Nott Bower
Head Constable

Bibliography

PART ONE: GENERAL BACKGROUND

Some students may be making a study of health, disease, or poverty through the ages, in which case invaluable background to the Victorian reign may be found in

1 Kitson Clark, G. *The Making of Victorian England*, Methuen 1962; or in
2 Young, G. M. *Victorian England: Portrait of an Age*, Oxford University Press 1936.

Those beginning a fuller survey of Victorian social reform will need to consult the admirable *Oxford Histories of England*, of which series the two relevant volumes are

3 Woodward, E. L. *The Age of Reform*, 1815–1870, Oxford University Press 1938, and
4 Ensor, R. C. K. *England, 1870–1914*, Oxford University Press 1936.

Books offering an analysis of the more specifically economic context include

5 Ashton, T. S. *The Industrial Revolution, 1760–1830*, Oxford University Press 1948: a neat concise introduction; and
6 Fay, C. R. *Great Britain, Adam Smith to the Present Day*, Longmans 1938: a substantial and pleasing account, revised now to 1949.
7 Cipolla, C. *A History of World Population*, Penguin 1962, is an up-to-date examination, complete with most interesting technological data, of the very meaningful factor of increasing population, while
8 Briggs, Asa. *Victorian Cities*, Odhams 1963, gives a fascinating insight into the growth of several major urban centres.

It is always worth while to consult

9 Webb, Sidney and Beatrice. *English Local Government* (1929),

reprinted Cass 1963, and in particular vols. 4, 6 and 8. This monumental and authoritative work has a sound index and it is possible to use it for speed and safety of reference. It has, of course, a predictable left-wing bias, in that, despite its dispassionate style, it earnestly favours social justice. In this it typifies a considerable amount of writing on nineteenth-century social problems, beginning with

10 Engels, F. *The Condition of the Working Classes, 1845* trans. W. O. Henderson and W. H. Chaloner, Blackwell 1958, and continuing with such characteristic works as

11 Tawney, R. A. *The Acquisitive Society*, Bell 1921; Penguin 1966; and

12 Hammond, J. L. and B. *The Black Age*, rev. edn. Penguin 1947.

NEW THINKING

With the aid of journals as well as books one can trace the controversy about nineteenth-century social administration. The seminal work is

13 Dicey, A. V. *Law and Public Opinion in England during the Nineteenth Century*, 2nd edn. Macmillan 1914, rev. 1962, in which the counterbalance of individualism and collectivism is most succinctly and precisely stated. A host of twentieth-century historians have laid siege to what they regard as a facile oversimplification.

14 MacDonagh, O. *A Pattern of Government Growth*, MacGibbon & Kee 1961;

15 —— 'Delegated legislation and administrative devolutions in the 1950s', *Victorian Studies* II (1955);

16 —— 'Nineteenth-century revolution in government', *Historical Journal* 1 (1958).

17 Lambert, R. J. *Sir John Simon*, MacGibbon & Kee 1964;

18 —— 'A Victorian national health service; State vaccination 1855–1871', *Historical Journal* 5 (1962);

19 Parris, H. 'Nineteenth-century revolution in government: a reappraisal reappraised', *Historical Journal* 3 (1960);

20 Brebuer, J. B. 'Laissez-faire and state intervention in nineteenth-century Britain', *Journal of Economic History* 8 (1948); and

21 Gutchen, R. M. 'Local improvements and centralisation in nineteenth-century England', *Historical Journal* 4 (1961): these are the chief protagonists, and they sustain a spirited and skilful campaign, arguing the presence of considerable administrative interference well before 1870. Some efforts have been made to redress the balance, notably in

22 Hart, J. 'Nineteenth-century social reform; a Tory interpretation of History', *Past and Present* 31 (1965).

Readers may also be interested in support for the view that there was relatively little action before 1870 in

23 Midwinter, E. C. 'A Tory interpretation of history, some comments', *Past and Present* 34 (1966), and

24 —— 'State intervention at local level; the new poor law in Lancashire', *Historical Journal* 10 (1967).

But for an urbane and well balanced viewpoint, especially of the mid-century years, students are advised to turn to

25 Burn, W. L. *The Age of Equipoise*, Allen & Unwin 1964.

Those interested in the philosophic lineage of social welfare would find in

26 Halévy, E. *The Growth of Philosophic Radicalism*, Faber 1924 (English trans. 1928), a scholarly and elegant investigation of the thought of Bentham and his confrères.

27 Finer, H. *The Theory and Practice of Modern Government*, Methuen 1950, astutely poses the problem of administrative application in modern society.

28 Bruce, M. *The Coming of the Welfare State*, Batsford 1961, is useful, especially its earlier sections, while a vigorous survey of Victorian ramifications on present day practice is given by

29 Roberts, D. *Victorian Origins of the British Welfare State*, New Haven, 1960. This book is indispensable for those wishing to judge the effects of Victorian social reform on social attitudes and administrative mechanisms today. It is second only to what is probably the most valuable book on Victorian Social reform:

30 Finer, S. E. *The Life and Times of Sir Edwin Chadwick*, Methuen 1952

PART TWO: MAIN DEVELOPMENTS

Works on the specialist topics here are difficult to recommend.

Bibliography

Some are slight primers; some are too austerely academic for the present purpose; some are outmoded; and some cover the topic as part of a general work on either the era or the topic. Apart from the Webbs (see **9** above) there is no sound book on the Victorian poor law. One must turn again to learned journals, among them

31 Beales, H. L. 'The New poor law', *History* (1931);
32 Roberts, D. 'How cruel was the Victorian poor law?' *Historical Journal* 6 (1963); and, for some very shrewd commentary on older views of the new poor law,
33 Blaug, M. 'The myth of the old poor law and the making of the new', *Journal of Economic History* 23 (1963), and
34 —— 'The Poor Law Report re-examined', *Journal of Economic History* 24 (1964).

Public health fares a little better, with

35 Frazer, W. M. *The History of English Public Health, 1834–1939*, Ballière, Tindall and Cox 1950, and
36 Lewis, R. A. *Edwin Chadwick and the Public Health Movement, 1832–1854*, Longmans 1952, providing excellent reviews of the general development and the origin of health services respectively.

R. J. Lambert's work (see **17** and **18** above) is particularly incisive and challenging, while

37 Holloway, S. W. F. 'Medical education in England, 1830–1858', *History* 49 (1964) and
38 Leff, S. *Social Medicine*, Routledge 1953, offer useful treatments of the medical aspects.
39 Briggs, Asa. 'Cholera and society in the nineteenth century', *Past and Present* 19 (1961) is an interesting commentary on the social aspects of cholera epidemics.

The clearest and most dependable introduction to police work is

40 Hart, J. M. *The British Police*, Allen & Unwin 1951.
41 Radzinowicz, *A History of English Criminal Law*, (vols. 2 and 3) Stevens 1956, is a massive but eminently fascinating and readable work.
42 Reith, C. *A New Study of Police History*, Oliver & Boyd 1956, is perhaps the most stimulating and unorthodox of the writings of this author, who has written several books on the police, especially the Metropolitan force.

For Robert ~~el's~~ part students should consult

43 Gash, N. *Mr Secretary Peel*, Longmans 1961, especially pp. 477–507.

44 Howard, D. L. *The English Prisons*, Methuen 1960, covers that aspect most satisfactorily.

One or two articles may be consulted, including

45 Hart, J. 'Reform of the Borough police 1835–56', *English Historical Review* 70 (1955);

46 —— 'The County and Borough Police Act, 1856', *Public Administration* 36 (1956); and

47 Parris, H. 'The Home Office and the provincial police in England and Wales, 1856–70', *Public Law* (1961).

It is always slightly surprising to discover that a relatively small amount of research and writing has been done on Victorian social amenities; hence the recourse to articles in learned journals. If, however, the student is tempted to dig out such articles he will normally find pointed and expert opinion, forcibly, briefly and clearly urged, and the experience gained from working the journals could prove most beneficial in any further studies.

Social life and reform is, of course, primarily local. It is to the local sources, which often serve as a vivid illustration of the national picture, that the reader should eventually go. Apart from parochial, county and town histories, there are dozens of local historical societies which have published papers on disease, crime and poverty in their own areas. Many libraries and municipal offices, large and small, keep old records and documents which are available for research purposes, nor must contemporary memoirs, diaries, newspapers and the novels of such authors as Charles Dickens, Charles Reade, Mrs Gaskell and Charles Kingsley be forgotten.   ·

48 *English Historical Documents*, vols. XII (I) and (II), general editor, D. Douglas; volume editors, G. M. Young and W. D. Handcock; Unwin 1956, would form a rich and proper start to such a search, and it is hoped that the extracts given in the Documents section of this book will prove helpful to those attracted by a desire to view the primary records.

Index

The Grammar Detective

Solving the Mysteries of Basic Grammar

Gillian Mary Hanson

Drawings by Mary Gillian Ward

continuum

Continuum

The Tower Building
11 York Road
London SE1 7NX

80 Maiden Lane, Suite 704
New York
NY 10038

British Library Cataloguing-in-Publication Data
A catalogue record for this book is available from the British Library.

ISBN: 978-08264-9807-6 (paperback)

Library of Congress Cataloging-in-Publication Data
A catalog record for this book is available from the Library of Congress.

Typeset by YHT Ltd, London
Printed and bound in Great Britain by MPG Books, Cornwall

Contents

Part Two: The Sentence

Part Three: Punctuation

Part Four: Usage

A Note to the Reader

The sometimes confusing and less than interesting rules of grammar can be quite daunting or mind numbing. Where does one begin? What does the general speaker, reader and writer of the English language really need to know as opposed to what would be more useful in the hands of professional linguists? Most people, it seems, would like to have some knowledge of the rudimentary elements of grammar but are unsure of how to begin and would agree that grammar can be a mystery. With this in mind, I have written *The Grammar Detective*, which presents you, the reader, with three small mysteries, each set at a carnival. You will build the solutions to these mysteries as you read the definitions of grammatical terms and work the exercises related to each one.

This book is written for all English-speaking people, and I have included explanations for both British English (BrE) and American English (AmE). The terms British English and American English are used in diverse ways by many people for different intentions, but for the purpose of this book, British English is used to refer to the commonly accepted rules of grammar that are used in the United Kingdom and other countries in which British English is spoken and American English for the United States and those countries which use American English. Most of these differences occur in the areas of spelling, pronunciation, some grammar, vocabulary and idioms. In general terms, a spelling used in Britain is more likely to be accepted in America than vice versa. In British English the spelling differs more frequently between homophones than it does in American English: *My bike keeps getting a flat tyre, and I'm tired of that.* (BrE) *My truck keeps getting a flat tire, and I'm tired of that.* (AmE): *May I write you a cheque? Yes, I think so. Let me check with the manager.* (BrE) *May I write you a check? Yes, I think so. Let me check with the manager.* (AmE): curb, as in *Please don't park your car so* *close to the <u>kerb</u>.* (BrE) *Please don't park your car so close to the <u>curb</u>.* (AmE) *Madam, please <u>curb</u> your temper!* (BrE) *Ma'am, please <u>curb</u> your temper!* (AmE) Differences in idiomatic meanings can often lead to humorous confusion; for instance, in British English '*Keep your pecker up*' is an admonition to be cheerful, but it has quite a different, rather vulgar, connotation in American English.

George Bernard Shaw quipped that England and America are 'two countries divided by a common language'; however, British and American English share far more similarities than differences; furthermore, according one writer, those people, '... with the English language at their common disposal, are connected more to each other than to the respective centers of their own countries.'* This is surely a cause for celebration and a reason to explore with renewed interest some of the basic elements of our colourful/colorful system of communication.

*Alan Sillitoe, preface to *An Across Walls Overview-Study of Novels and Short Stories by Eighteen Twentieth-Century English and American Authors*

The Mystery in the Hall of Mirrors

(1) Gabby and Tim, her brother, are visiting the Carnival of Grammar. (2) They stop outside the Hall of Mirrors, next to the Fake 'n' Fun toy booth and the House of Horrors, which is featuring the role of the 'Screaming Corpse'.

(3) 'Shall we go in?' Tim asks.

(4) 'Sure,' answers Gabby, 'but let's leave the door open.'

(5) Inside, they laugh hysterically as they view themselves in the many contorting mirrors. (6) At times, Gabby looks ten feet tall and as emaciated as Don Quixote, whereas Tim looks very short and as chubby as Sancho Panza. (7) Their bodies divide and multiply as if by magic; their faces grow long and at other times broad. (8) When they pause for breath in front of one mirror, Tim sees something behind his back. (9) At first, he thinks it might be part of his own reflection, but then he realizes it is a stranger – a woman who is lying on the floor with a knife in her back!

(10) 'Look!' Tim clutches Gabby's arm and points shakily into the mirror. (11) 'Over there.'

(12) Gabby gasps with horror. (13) 'What shall we do?' she whispers, almost collapsing herself.

(14) 'We have to call the police,' replies Tim.

(15) Gabby agrees. (16) 'Let's find a phone.'

(17) Within minutes, a police car arrives, driven by Officer Bloggs, the carnival's assigned policeman. (18) The wail of its siren draws a large crowd which, impelled by the thought of imminent danger or perhaps even death, pushes its way through a flock of pigeons and surges forward.

(19) Officer Bloggs holds up his hand and addresses the crowd. (20) 'Wait outside, please. (21) I'll have none of you running in.' (22) Gabby and Tim take Officer Bloggs into the Hall of Mirrors.

(23) The body has vanished!

(24) 'Oh, no,' shrieks Gabby.

(25) 'I swear the woman was right here,' avows Tim. (26) 'She was lying on the ground with a knife stuck in her back.'

(26) 'Possibly a corpse?' asks Officer Bloggs.

(27) 'It certainly looked like one,' answers Gabby.

(28) For a moment Officer Bloggs not only twirls his moustaches but also

rocks back on his heels. (29) 'Let me reflect a moment . . . I'm afraid this could be murder.'

What do you think?

Part One: Parts of Speech

A part of speech may be defined as a grammatical unit or class of words generally categorized in eight parts: noun, pronoun, verb, adjective, adverb, preposition, conjunction and interjection. Many of the words in these categories function as more than one part of speech: *Tim* <u>*booked*</u> (verb) *two tickets for the Hall of Mirrors while Gabby was reading her* <u>*book*</u> (noun) *on botanical illustrations.*

Nouns

Nouns are parts of speech that identify people, places, ideas, things and qualities. A noun may be used in a variety of sentence functions, usually in combination with the definite or indefinite article and modifiers. In a noun phrase, a noun functions as the main or only word. It can be the subject, direct object, indirect object, subject complement, object complement, complement of a preposition, or modifier of another noun. If the noun is singular but represents a group of people, the verb is singular in American English: *Fifty per cent of the crowd is eating toffee apples. The crowd is indifferent to the cries of the carnival barker.* In British English the verb may be also plural if referring to each particular member or item in the group: *Fifty per cent of the crowd are eating toffee apples. The crowd are indifferent to the cries of the carnival barker.* If the noun is plural, the verb is singular: *People like the carnival.* Unlike Latin, modern English makes only two case distinctions: common case (tiger) and possessive/genitive case (tiger's). All nouns are either common or proper. Proper nouns always begin with a capital (BrE)/upper case (AmE) letter and may be either singular or plural. Proper nouns name specific people, places and things: *Tim, Gabby, the Carnival of Grammar, Beatrice's Bearded Ladies, the Greasy Spoon Café.*

Before visiting the carnival to see <u>Beatrice's Bearded Ladies</u>, <u>Tim</u> and <u>Gabby</u> eat fish and chips at the <u>Greasy Spoon Cafe</u>.

Practice: Write a sentence that contains at least two *proper nouns*:

1.

Common nouns name general things and always begin with lower case letters. Common nouns may be either singular or plural: *music, violin, shadows, finger, folds, curtain*:

The eerie <u>music</u> of the <u>violin</u> came floating from the <u>shadows</u> where a <u>finger</u> beckoned to them from the <u>folds</u> of the dark <u>curtain</u>.

 Practice: Write a sentence that contains at least three *common nouns*:

1.

Nouns may be further classified as countable or uncountable (BrE)/ non-countable (AmE), concrete or abstract, animate or inanimate, collective and compound. A noun may be classified under one or more of these terms. A noun may also have one feature in one context and the opposite feature in another: *This <u>room</u> is full of mirrors. Make <u>room</u> for me in front of that mirror.*
Countable or uncountable (BrE)/non-countable (AmE):
Countable nouns may be singular or plural in number. This distinction is generally indicated by a difference between singular and plural forms: *tiger/tigers, phenomenon/phenomena* (uncountable).
Countable/noncountable nouns have only one form: air, peace.

 Practice: Write two sentences that contain one countable noun and one uncountable (BrE)/non-countable (AmE) noun:

1.

2.

Concrete nouns are countable and name objects that can be identified through one or more of the five senses (sight, sound, smell, touch, taste): *candyfloss, ice, lights, screams, Ferris wheel*:

The metal safety <u>bar</u> felt like <u>ice</u>, and the sweet <u>candyfloss</u> melted in their <u>mouths</u> as <u>Tim</u> and <u>Gabby</u> rode the <u>Ferris wheel</u> up into the glittering <u>lights</u>; then, their <u>screams</u> rent the night <u>air</u> as they plummeted back into the <u>smell</u> of <u>hot dogs</u> and <u>fried onions</u>.

 Practice: Write two sentences containing at least three concrete nouns:

1.

2.

Abstract nouns are often uncountable (BrE)/non-countable (AmE) although some may be plural and some may be both. These nouns name qualities or ideas: *fear, excitement, nausea, dizziness, exuberance,* etc.:

The <u>excitement</u> (u/c) over, <u>fear</u> (u/c) and <u>exuberance</u> (u) were replaced by distinct feelings of <u>nausea</u> (u) and <u>dizziness</u> (u) as Tim and Gabby stumbled away from the Ferris wheel.

 Practice: Write two sentences containing abstract nouns:

1.

2.

Animate or inanimate nouns are nouns that may have a male or female reference: father, boy, mother, girl, etc. Some pairs of nouns mark male/female contrast with a suffix: host/hostess, hero/ heroine, usher/usherette, widow/widower, etc. Animate nouns that are gender specific are no longer deemed politically correct and have often been replaced by other nouns: ring master/ring person; postman/mail carrier; chairman/chairperson; mankind/ humankind; policeman/police officer, etc. The gender reference of human nouns becomes clear when the pronouns *he/his* or *she/ hers* relate to the noun: *My friend likes mustard with his hot dog, but my other friend prefers mayonnaise with hers.* Non-human animate nouns allow male, female, or non-gender reference: *Don't touch the tiger;*

he/she/it might bite. Inanimate nouns are lifeless and are the most common form of nouns: *Ferris wheel, tent, scream,* etc.

 Practice: Write three sentences that contain both animate and inanimate nouns:

1.

2.

3.

Collective nouns are nouns that name groups of persons or things: *crowd, audience, group, herd, team,* etc.:

The group outside the candy-apples booth soon grew to a large crowd when a team from the Health Department came by to inspect the tooth marks in the apples made by a passing herd of miniature horses.

 Practice: Write a sentence that contains at least two collective nouns:

1.

Compound nouns are nouns that consist of one or more words that function as a single noun. They may or may not be hyphenated: *coconut stall, exit sign, brother-in-law, hot dogs, bus stop,* etc.:

After borrowing some money from their brother-in-law, Tim and Gabby caught the bus and arrived at the bus stop for the carnival just as the man who ran the coconut stall began to sing: 'There stands my wife; the idol of my life, roll-a-bowl-a-ball-a-penny-a-pitch.'

 Practice: Write a sentence that contains at least two *compound nouns*:

1.

You are the grammar detective:

To solve the mystery in the Hall of Mirrors:

Circle all of the nouns that appear in the story

Clue: Nouns are parts of speech that name people, places, ideas, things and qualities, and may be common or proper, singular or compound.

Check your nouns against the following list:

> arm, back, bodies, body, breath, brother, Carnival of Grammar, corpse, crowd, danger, death, Don Quixote, door, faces, Fake 'n Fun toy booth, feet, flock of pigeons, floor, Gabby, ground, Hall of Mirrors, hand, heels, horror, House of Horrors, knife, magic, minutes, mirrors, moment, murder moustaches, Officer Bloggs, part, phone, police, policeman, police car, reflection, role, Sancho Panza, Screaming Corpse, siren, stranger, Tim, thought, wail, way, woman

Choose the nouns to complete the solution:
There is no _____ (noun)! _____ (proper noun) and _____ (proper noun) do see a _____ (noun) who is lying on the _____ (noun), and she does have a _____ (noun) in her _____ (noun), but it is the woman from the _____ (proper compound noun) next door. She plays the _____ (noun) of the _____ (proper compound noun) and ends her _____ (noun) by running outside with a _____ (noun) from the _____ (proper noun)

toy booth stuck in her back and collapsing on the _____
noun). _____ (proper noun) sees her in the many contorting
_____ (noun) which reflect the open _____ (noun) of the
_____ (proper noun) imminent, Impelled by the _____
(noun) of _____ (noun) or perhaps even _____ (noun), she
disappears as if by _____ (noun) behind his _____ (noun) to
return to the _____ (proper compound noun).

(Solution on page 133)

The Mystery in the Ghost Tunnel

(1) Jinx and Jason are also visiting the carnival. (2) After much persuasion, Jinx agrees to take a ride on the Ghost Train with Jason; however, distant shrieks from the tunnel's dark mouth almost convince her otherwise.

(3) 'Come on, Jinx,' urges Jason. (4) 'How scary can it be? (5) It's all fake. (6) And, look! (7) We'll be safe.' (8) He points to the stoic figure of Officer Bloggs who is standing close by, absentmindedly twirling his moustaches.

(9) 'All right,' Jinx replies.

(10) The two purchase their tickets from a ghostlike figure, who sits grinning in its cobweb-festooned booth, and climb into their seat. (11) Several minutes elapse before the little train shudders into action along the tracks and is swallowed up by the tunnel.

(12) 'We're off,' observes Jason.

(13) Jinx glances around with trepidation. (14) I wish we were off this ride, she thinks. (15) She notices a friend, Fleur, who is sitting with a companion a few seats behind. (16) She waves and is rewarded by a nervous wave from her friend.

(17) The tunnel feels cold and damp as the train picks up speed. (18) 'I hope it doesn't malfunction,' says Jinx, leaning close to Jason. (19) The train slows down as it comes to a bend in the tunnel. (20) A skeletal hand shoots out of the wall. (21) Jinx is terrified and tries to avoid it; then, she glances behind her. (22) Fleur and her companion have disappeared! (23) Where are they?

(24) 'That is weird,' says Jason. (25) 'They couldn't have jumped off the train.' (26) He spreads his arms and touches the dark sides of the tunnel to prove his theory.

(27) Jinx shivers. (28) 'This is horrible. (29) What if something awful has happened to them?' she asks as the train emerges from the tunnel and comes to a halt.

(30) Jason laughs. (31) 'Come on, Jinx. (32) I'm sure it is not such a mystery. (33) You usually like this kind of stuff. (34) Remember, it's just a game, and Officer Bloggs is just there. (35) We can tell him what's happened.'

What do you think?

Verbs

A verb denotes the action in a sentence. Without a main verb the sentence does not exist; it is incomplete and often called a fragment (AmE). The main verb gives life to the sentence. Even though many verbs share the same base forms as nouns (*laugh, dance, cry,* etc.), they comprise a distinct word class. There are two principal types of verbs: the main verb and the auxiliary verb. Main verbs are classified as regular or irregular. Auxiliary verbs are classified as primary auxiliaries (*be, have, do*) or modal verbs (*may, can, will, shall, must, ought, need, dare*). Regular verbs have five forms: the base or infinitive form; the past tense form; the past participle form; the present participle form and the −s form:

Base Form	Past Tense	Past Participle	Present Participle	−s form
(to) scream	*screamed*	*screamed*	*screaming*	*screams*
(to) laugh	*laughed*	*laughed*	*laughing*	*laughs*

Gabby likes to scream when she rides through the Ghost Tunnel.
Gabby screamed in delicious horror as she rode through the Ghost Tunnel.
Gabby's throat was sore because she had screamed so much when she rode through the Ghost Tunnel.
Gabby is laughing as she tries to catch the bobbing duck.
Gabby laughs delightedly as she tries to catch the bobbing duck.

 Practice: Write the same sentence four times, using a different verb form for each:

1.

2.

3.

4.

Irregular verbs do not follow the same pattern that regular verbs do. There are quite a few irregular verbs, and you may find a list of them in the dictionary. The most commonly used irregular verb is *to be*:

Base form	*(to) be*
Past tense	*was/were*
Past participle	*been*
Present participle	*being*
Present tense	*am/is/are*

Other irregular verbs include:

Base Form	Past Tense	Past Participle	Present Participle	–s form
(to) drink	*drank*	*drunk*	*drinking*	*drinks*
(to) sing	*sang*	*sung*	*singing*	*sings*
(to) swim	*swam*	*swum*	*swimming*	*swims*
(to) lie	*lay*	*lain*	*lying*	*lies*
(to) lay	*laid*	*laid*	*laying*	*lays*

The most commonly *misused* irregular verbs are '*lie*' and '*lay*'. '*Lie*' means '*to recline*' and does not need to take a direct object. '*Lay*' means '*to place*' or '*to put*' and must have a direct object to complete the meaning of the sentence:

After much excitement, Gabby likes to <u>lie</u> on the floor.
Exhausted, Gabby <u>lay</u> on the floor.
Gabby <u>had lain</u> on the floor for a few minutes before she felt refreshed enough to go with Tim to the Hall of Mirrors.

 Practice: Write three sentences that contain three forms of the verb *to lie*:

1.

2.

3.

Tim <u>lay</u> his hand on the head of the miniature dancing dog.
Tim <u>laid</u> his hand on the head of the miniature dancing dog.
Until it began to growl, Tim <u>had laid</u> his hand on the head of the
miniature dancing dog.

Practice: Write three sentences that contain three forms of the verb *to lay*:

1.

2.

3.

Use of Verb Tenses

Use the present tense if you want to describe an action that is taking place as you write about it or if you want to describe an action that takes place regularly:

Present: *Tim <u>guffaws</u> along with the mechanical laughing policeman.*

Tim <u>guffaws</u> every time he hears the mechanical laughing policeman.

Practice: Write the same sentence twice to describe an action that is taking place as you write about it and an action that takes place regularly:

1.

2.

Use the past tense if you want to describe an action that has already taken place: *Tim <u>guffawed</u> along with the mechanical laughing policeman.*

Practice: Write a sentence that describes an action that has already taken place:

1.

Other tenses are formed with the addition of another verb such as the future tense, the perfect tense and the progressive (or continuous) tense. Use the future tense to describe an action that has not yet taken place:

Tim <u>will guffaw</u> when he hears the mechanical laughing policeman.

Practice: Write a sentence that describes an action that will occur in the future:

1.

Use the perfect tenses: present perfect, past perfect *and* future perfect, to describe actions that were completed or will be completed before other actions in the sentence. The perfect tenses use a form of the verb 'to have' with the past participle. Use the present perfect tense to indicate an action that began in the past and continues in the present *or* an action that began in the past and ended in the present:

Tim <u>had been eating</u> hamburgers for an hour.
Gabby <u>has finished</u> her candyfloss.

Practice: Write a sentence that describes an action that began in the past and continues in the present:

1.

Practice: Write a sentence that contains an action that began in the past and ended in the present:

1.

Use the past perfect tense to describe an action that took place before a certain time in the past:

By twelve midnight, Tim and Gabby <u>had decided</u> to go home.

Practice: Write a sentence that describes an action that took place before a certain time in the past:

1.

Use the future perfect tense to describe an action that will be completed in the future:
By twelve midnight, Tim and Gabby <u>will have exhausted</u> all of their energy.

Practice: Write a sentence that describes an action that will be completed in the future:

1.

Use the progressive (continuous) tenses: present progressive, past progressive, future progressive, present perfect progressive, past perfect progressive and future perfect progressive, to describe a continuing action. The progressive tenses use a form of the verb *to be* with the present participle. Use the present progressive to describe an action that is taking place at the time you are writing about it:
The carnival lights <u>are flickering</u> wildly.

Practice: Write a sentence that describes an action that is taking place at the time you are writing about it:

1.

Use the past progressive tense to describe a past continuing action or to describe an action that takes place simultaneously with any past action:
Tim and Gabby <u>were feeling</u> quite shattered when they stepped off the bumper cars.
Even though he <u>was feeling</u> nauseous, Tim was craving another ride.

Practice: Write a sentence that describes a past continuing action and a sentence that describes an action that takes place at the same time as another past action:

1.

2.

Use the future progressive tense to describe a continuing action in the future:

Tim <u>will soon be regretting</u> his rash decision to ride the bumper cars again.

 Practice: Write a sentence that describes a continuing action in the future:

1.

Use the present perfect progressive to describe an action that began in the past and continues in the present with the probability of continuing in the future:

Tim and Gabby <u>have been riding</u> the bumper cars for fifty minutes.

 Practice: Write a sentence that describes an action that began in the past and continues in the present with the probability of continuing in the future:

1.

Use the past perfect progressive to describe a past action that continued until another action took its place:

Before Tim and Gabby rode on the Big Dipper, they <u>had been exploring</u> the Fake 'n' Fun toy booth.

 Practice: Write a sentence that describes a past action that continued until another action took its place:

1.

Use the future perfect progressive to describe an action that will continue until a certain time in the future:

By midnight, Tim and Gabby <u>will have been enjoying</u> the carnival for six hours.

Practice: Write a sentence that describes an action that will continue until a certain time:

1.

Linking Verbs

A linking verb is a verb that does not describe an action. All linking verbs are linked to a subject and a subject complement, which can be one word or several words. The subject complement is either a predicate noun if it identifies the subject, or a predicate adjective if it describes the subject. The most common linking verb is *to be*: *am, is, are, was, were*. *Tim is Gabby's older brother* (identifies the subject). Other linking verbs include *seem, appear, look, happy, feel, become*, etc.: *Gabby seems happy riding the unicorn* (describes the subject).

Practice: Write two sentences that contain linking/copulative verbs:

1.

2.

Transitive and Intransitive Verbs

Verbs which are not linking verbs are either transitive or intransitive verbs.

A transitive verb is one that requires a direct object:
Gabby gave Tim her hot dog (direct object: hot dog).
The Spider Woman adjusted her arms (direct object: arms).

Practice: Write a sentence that contains a transitive verb:

1.

An intransitive verb does not take a direct object:
Tim gazed.
Gabby shuddered.

Practice: Write a sentence that contains an *intransitive verb*:

1.

Infinitives

Infinitive forms of verbs are the base form + to: *to sing, to despair, to laugh*.

Infinitives never take the place of the main verb in a sentence; rather, they depend on the tense of the main verb:

Tim and Gabby went (main verb) to see the Leaping Lizard Man.

Tim and Gabby would like (main verb) to have seen the Leaping Lizard Man.

 Practice: Write a sentence that contains an *infinitive*:

1.

Participles

Participle forms of verbs also depend on the tense of the main verb in the sentence to form their tenses. Use the present participle form to describe an action that takes place at the same time as the main verb:

Wiping the mustard from his chin, Tim followed Gabby into the Hall of Mirrors.

 Practice: Write a sentence that contains a *present participle*:

1.

Use the past participle or the present perfect participle form to describe an action that took place before the action of the main verb:

Having wiped the mustard from his chin, Tim followed Gabby into the Hall of Mirrors.

Practice: Write a sentence that uses a *present perfect participle* and a sentence that contains a *past participle*:

1.

2.

Mood

If you want to express a statement, ask a question, give a command, express a desire, or a contradiction, use the mood form of a verb. Mood forms are either indicative, imperative, or subjunctive. Use the indicative mood to describe an opinion, to state a fact, or to ask a question:

The spicy chili dog <u>must have had</u> a profound effect on Gabby's stomach.
The spicy chili dog <u>had</u> a profound effect on Gabby's stomach.
Did the spicy chili dog <u>have</u> a profound effect on Gabby's stomach?

Practice: Write three sentences that contain the indicative mood:

1.

2.

3.

Use the imperative mood to give a command or to state a direct request. Usually, the imperative mood takes the base form of the verb only and does not include the subject:

<u>Give</u> me two hot dogs, please!
<u>Pass</u> along the line, please!

Practice: Write two sentences that contain the imperative mood:

1.

2.

The present subjunctive uses the base form of the verb. Use the present subjunctive mood in clauses which begin with '*that*' and are preceded by words such as '*insisted*', '*asked*', '*agreed*', '*demanded*', '*requested*', '*denied*' and '*recommended*': *Gabby demanded <u>that they stay</u>. Tim, however, insisted <u>that they leave</u>.*

Practice: Write two sentences in the *present subjunctive* mood:

1.

2.

The past subjunctive takes the same form as the past tense of the verb.

Use the past subjunctive mood to describe something that is contrary to fact in a statement that begins with '*if*', or to express a desire:

Tim felt as if he <u>were</u> in charge and insisted they leave. (contrary to fact)
Gabby wished she <u>were staying</u> for a little while longer. (desire)
'If mother <u>were</u> here,' exclaimed Tim hotly, 'she would make you leave.' (contrary to fact)
'All right, don't act as if you <u>were</u> about to have kittens,' replied Gabby smartly. (contrary to fact)
'I wish you <u>were</u> a little more respectful,' said Tim pompously. (desire)

Practice: Write two sentences in the *past subjunctive* mood:

1.

2.

Voice

Voice may be either active or passive. To describe the action of the subject in a sentence, use the active voice: *Gabby and Tim* (subjects) <u>*bought*</u> *their bus tickets* (direct objects).

Practice: Write a sentence in the *active voice*:

1.

If the subject of the verb is acted upon rather than performing the action, use the passive voice. In the passive voice, the direct object in the sentence becomes the subject:

The bus tickets (subjects) <u>*were bought*</u> *by Tim and Gabby.*

Note: Because it is direct and concise, it is usually more effective to use the active voice in your writing.

Modal Auxiliary Verbs

Modal auxiliary verbs are often called helping verbs because they go along with the main verb to indicate possibility, future action, permission, desire, capability, necessity, etc. Modal auxiliaries include: *can, could, may, might, must* and *ought*:

'As the last bus leaves at twelve midnight, we <u>must</u> leave the carnival by then,' insisted Tim.

'I <u>might</u> not be ready,' answered Gabby.

'You <u>ought</u> to be,' Tim replied briskly, *'or you <u>could</u> be walking home.'*

Practice: Write three sentences that contain *modal auxiliaries*:

1.

2.

3.

You are the grammar detective:

To solve the mystery concerning the ghost in the tunnel, turn to the story and:

Circle all of the main verbs
Clue: these may be regular verbs or linking verbs
Check the words you have circled with the verb list below:

agrees, am, are, avoid, be, bend, can, climb, comes, convinces, couldn't, desists, disappeared, doesn't, elapse, emerges, enters, feels, glances, grinning, happened, has, have, is, laughs, leads, like, look, notices, observes, picks, points, purchase, replies, rewarded, says, seated, shivers, shoots, shudders, sitting, slows, spreads, standing, sure, swallowed, tell, terrified, thinks, touches, twirling, urges, visiting, waves, we'll, we're, wish

Now add the missing verbs to complete the solution:

Fleur and her companion _____ (verb) down to _____ (verb) the skeletal hand that _____ (verb) out of the wall in the bend in the tunnel. Jinx _____ (verb) around with trepidation. The two seem to have been swallowed up by the tunnel; however, it ____ (linking verb) not what she _____ (verb)! Officer Bloggs observes the situation and _____ (linking verb) up with an idea. He _____ (verb) in twirling his moustaches, and, to prove his theory, he _____(verb) the tunnel's dark mouth and ____ (verb) out the terrified friends who have been sitting in the dark for several minutes, and the mystery _____ (linking verb) is solved: when the Ghost Train came to a halt, only the section in which Jinx and Jason were _____ (verb) emerged from the tunnel due to a malfunction in the tracks.

(Solution on page 133)

The Mystery at the Carousel

(1) Emma, who is three years old, is very excited. (2) This is her first visit to the carnival! (3) Her parents, Ben and Cecy, have brought her. (4) All three are standing in front of the carousel. (5) Beside the carousel stands an easel bearing a cryptic message that reads 'O. O. O.'(6) Emma watches the animals spinning slowly around: a large chicken with a fine red comb, a sly fox with yellow eyes, a lamb with a lavender collar, a small ginger-coloured giraffe, a small, pink hippo and a grey donkey. (7) Each animal smiles enigmatically. (8) Emma claps her hands with great glee.

(9) 'Me go!' she shouts.

(10) Cecy laughs, 'All right.'

(11) 'Will she be safe?' asks Ben.

(12) 'Yes. I think so. It's just for little children.'

(13) 'OK. Com'on Emma.' (14) Ben swings Emma up in the air as the carousel comes to a halt. (15) 'Which animal would you like to sit on?'

(16) Emma points to the small pink hippo.

(17) 'Right!' (18) Ben places Emma on the hippo's broad back and fastens the safety strap around her.

(19) 'Where do we pay?' wonders Cecy, looking around for the attendant, a thwarted disc jockey/stand-up comedian who is hiding behind the easel and smiling maliciously.

(20) 'I don't see anyone,' says Ben.

(21) 'No other passengers either.'

(22) The music begins; the carousel starts its slow revolutions. (23) Emma chuckles happily.

(24) As Ben walks beside the carousel, the music changes. (25) A cacophony of animal voices takes over. (26) 'Hear that, Emma! (27) The animals talk.'

(28) 'Funny.'

(29) 'Yes, it is funny. (30) This hippo's yelping like a fox.' (31) Ben wonders what the reason could be and notices Officer Bloggs emerging from a group of bystanders that has gathered. (32) 'Officer!' he calls. (33) 'Something is wrong here.' (34) Officer Bloggs twirls his moustaches as he listens to the noises. (35) Strange, he thinks. (36) The donkey is clucking like a chicken; this pink hippo is bleating like a lamb; the chicken with the fine red comb is bellowing like a hippo and the small ginger-coloured giraffe is braying like a donkey!

(37) 'All of these animals are out of order,' he pronounces as he stands next to the easel.

(38) 'I think the sound tape of the animals' voices is mixed up,' says Ben.
(39) 'We need to get to the bottom of this.'

(40) The attendant smiles cunningly.

What do you think?

Adjectives and Adverbs

Adjectives are words that modify nouns or pronouns and complement linking verbs such as 'be' and 'seem'. While most adjectives are always used before a noun, others always follow the noun they describe: 'thrills and spills *galore*'. Adjectives nearly always come after linking verbs: 'Jinx is *happy*.'

The <u>black</u> tent stood next to the Hall of Mirrors.
A <u>greasy</u> hot dog lay in Tim's hand.
<u>Loud</u> music from the <u>swirling</u> roundabout filled the <u>night</u> air.
The Spider Woman, <u>plump and hirsute</u>, sighs gently.

 Practice: Write three sentences that contain three different uses of adjectives:

1.

2.

3.

Adverbs are words that modify verbs, adjectives, or other adverbs. Most adverbs are formed by adding *-ly* as in *suddenly, playfully*. Some are formed from nouns in combination with other suffixes: *-wise* as in *clockwise, lengthwise*, and *-ward* as in *northward, skyward*. A set of common adverbs have no suffixes: *here, there, now, just, well*, though some are compounds: *therefore, nevertheless*. Use adverbs to describe verbs, adjectives, other adverbs, phrases, clauses and sentences:

Two of the Spider Woman's arms waved <u>energetically</u> in the night air.
Gabby clung <u>heroically</u> to the mane of her colourful unicorn.
The roundabout spun <u>recklessly</u> in a kaleidoscope of music, warmth and colour.

Practice: Write three sentences that contain three different uses of adverbs:

1.

2.

3.

Note: Many adverbs end in *-ly*. However, if a word does end with the *-ly* suffix, it does not necessarily mean it is an adverb:
*'Lovely (*adjective*) Gabby, her hair flying, waved gaily (*adverb*) to Tim as she sped by on her comely (*adjective*) unicorn.'*
Both adjectives and adverbs may be positive, comparative, or superlative.
Some adverbs:

Positive	Comparative	Superlative
well	*better*	*best*
sly	*slyer*	*slyest*
ravenously	*more ravenously*	*most ravenously*

Some adjectives:

Positive	Comparative	Superlative
happy	*happier*	*happiest*
scared	*more scared*	*most scared*
gaudy	*gaudier*	*gaudiest*
bad	*worse*	*worst*

Use a positive adjective or adverb to describe an attribute:
It was a <u>bad</u> night for unicorns.
The unicorns frolicked <u>poorly</u> that night.

Practice: Write a sentence that describes an attribute of a noun and a sentence that describes an attribute of a verb:

1.

2.

Use a comparative adjective or adverb to describe two things or two actions:
It was a <u>worse</u> night for unicorns than for flying pigs.
The unicorns frolicked <u>more poorly</u> than the flying pigs.

Practice: Write a sentence that compares two things and a sentence that compares two actions:

1.

2.

Use a superlative adjective or adverb to compare three or more things or actions:
It was the <u>worst</u> night (of many) *for unicorns.*
The unicorns frolicked the <u>most poorly</u> that night. (than many other times)

Practice: Write a sentence in which you compare three or more things and a sentence in which you compare three or more actions:

1.

2.

You are the grammar detective:

To solve the Mystery at the Carousel, turn to the story and:

Circle all of the adjectives and adverbs

Clue: an adjective describes a noun and an adverb describes a verb

Check your words with the list below:

> amateur, animal, awful, broad, cunningly, crytic,
> enigmatically, fine, first, ginger-coloured, grey, great,

happily, large, lavender, little, maliciously, pink, red, slow,
slowly, sly, small, thwarted, unsuspecting, very, yellow

Now choose the missing adjectives and adverbs to complete the
solution:

The attendant, a _____ (adjective) disc jockey and an
_____ (adjective) stand-up comedian, has _____
(adverb) mixed up the carousel sound tape of the animals' voices to
confuse his patrons and left behind a _____ (adjective) message
on the easel that reads 'O.O.O.': out of order. He grins _____
(adverb) and watches Ben and Cecy's confusion with great glee.
Officer Bloggs, however, looks from the sign to the attendant and
smiles _____ (adverb) as he twirls his moustaches. 'I think we
can get to the bottom of this. The reason for this cacophony is,' he
points at the grinning man, 'this attendant is a ____ (adjective) fox
who enjoys playing tricks on his (adjective) _____ patrons.'

(Solution on page 134)

Determiners

A determiner is a word that limits a noun or a noun phrase. Primary determiners are mutually exclusive and contrast with adjectives, with which, however, they can concur: *the* best candyfloss, *no* place for the faint of heart. The most common kind of determiner is the article, which is either definite *the* or indefinite *a* or *an*. Use *a* before consonants. Use *an* before words that begin with vowels: *an exciting play* or words that begin with silent consonants: *The bus bore them homeward. A bus bore them homeward. A bus, not an airplane, bore them homeward.* Use *the* to refer to something specific or something you have already mentioned: *They boarded the bus that would take them home.* Use *a* to refer to something general: *They boarded a bus.*

 Practice: Write three sentences using three different articles:

1.

2.

3.

Other primary determiners include: demonstratives such as *this* or *those*: *Those hot dogs smell good*; possessives: *my, your*: *My hat and your umbrella have purple polka dots*; and quantifiers such as: *each, every, no, any, some*: *No laughter was heard in the Ghost Tunnel although some people screamed.*

Secondary determiners may be placed before or after the primary determiner. Those placed before the primary determiner often refer to quantity, such as *all, both, half*: *all of this hamburger, both your candy apples, half her hot dog*; double: *double the fun*; twice: *twice as exciting*; *once*: *the elephant is fed* <u>*once*</u> *every day*. Fractions: *that plush toy is not worth* <u>*a quarter*</u> *of the price I paid for it*. *Such* and *what* in exclamations also come before the primary determiner: *It was* <u>*such*</u> *a waste of money, but* <u>*what*</u> *a good time we had!* Those secondary determiners placed after the primary determiner include numbers and some quantifiers: *These* <u>*two*</u> *giraffes look even thinner than the rest. This is my* <u>*first*</u> *time at the carnival.* <u>*Many*</u> *pigeons flew over the Hall of Mirrors.* <u>*Several*</u> *pigeons were rather portly.*

 Practice: Write three sentences containing different determiners:

1.

2.

3.

Determiners may also be divided according to the countability of the nouns they modify. With singular countable nouns use: *a/an, each, every, either, neither, this, that*:
I have enough money to buy <u>*either a*</u> *toffee apple or* <u>*an*</u> *exciting ride on the bumper cars.* <u>*This*</u> *elephant looks more comfortable than* <u>*that*</u> *camel.*

 Practice: Write three sentences containing determiners with single countable nouns:

1.

2.

3.

With uncountable (BrE)/non-countable (AmE) nouns use: *much, little/a little*, and *less, least*: <u>*Much*</u> *has been discussed about the disappearance of the sword swallower, but the* <u>*least*</u> *said the better.*

 Practice: Write three sentences containing determiners with uncountable/non-countable nouns:

1.

2.

3.

With plural countable nouns use: *all, enough, more, most, a lot, lots of, some* and *any*.
More people flock to the carnival at the weekends although some do come during the week.

 Practice: Write three sentences containing determiners with plural countable nouns:

1.

2.

3.

With countable plurals use: *a few, few, fewer, fewest, both, many, several, these, those* and *numbers*. *Those who come will not regret it, and few leave dissatisfied.*

 Practice: Write three sentences containing determiners and countable plurals:

1.

2.

3.

With most common nouns use: *the, no,* possessives and some '*wh*' words:
The note on the door says 'Enter at your own risk' with no hint of what lies behind it except a sketch of a small man minus his left eye, so at what time and where should we line up for the tickets?

 Practice: Write three sentences containing three different determiners and common nouns:

1.

2.

3.

Pronouns

A pronoun is a conventional part of speech that functions most often like a noun, as the subject of a sentence, which is called the *pronoun antecedent*, and is generally a substitute for a noun or noun phrase. Careful use of pronouns eliminates needless repetition by providing a cohesive element in discourse:

Tim looked nervously over <u>his</u> shoulder at the majestic-looking midget <u>who</u> seemed to be following <u>him</u>.

Rather than:

Tim looked nervously over Tim's shoulder at the majestic-looking midget who seemed to be following Tim.

Pronouns are classified by three cases: *nominative* (BrE)/*subjective* (AmE), which is usually the subject of a sentence: *<u>I</u> lost my cool in the Ghost Tunnel*; *accusative* (BrE)/*objective* (AmE), which functions as the object of a verb or a preposition: *<u>You</u> lost your cool in the Ghost Tunnel*; and *genitive* (BrE)/*possessive* (AmE), which usually indicates ownership: *Gabby lost <u>her</u> cool in the Ghost Tunnel.*

Nominative/ subjective	accusative/ objective	genitive/ possessive
I	me	my, mine
you	you	your, yours
he	him	his
she	her	her, hers
it	it	its
we	us	our, ours
you	you	your, yours
they	them	their, theirs

There are eight kinds of pronouns: personal, interrogative, indefinite, relative, demonstrative, reciprocal, reflexive and intensive.

Personal pronouns represent people and are either first, second or third person:

I ate the candy apple.
He or she ate the candy apple.
We ate the candy apples.
She and he rode the rocking raft through the Aqua Angst ride.
When they didn't reappear, I became concerned about their safety.
We summoned our courage and began to look for them.
We found they had been caught up in the jaws of a mechanical shark, but, fortunately, they were safe.

 Practice: Write three related sentences that contain *personal pronouns*:

1.

2.

3.

Interrogative pronouns are used in questions: who, whom, which, what, whose?
Note: Who/whom: Use the pronoun *whom* as the object of a preposition or the object of a verb. Use the pronoun *who* as the subject or subject complement of a sentence.
Who screamed?
Is this the gypsy to whom I am related?

Whom did they invite into their tent?
What is in that colourful tent?
Whose spotted owl is this?
Which one of the venues do you find the most entertaining?

Practice: Write five short sentences that contain one of each of the five *interrogative pronouns*:

1.

2.

3.

4.

5.

Indefinite pronouns do not refer to any specific person or thing: one, someone, anyone, everyone, no one, nobody, several, each, all, neither, either, both, many, few, any, some, etc.:

Several sideshows displayed bright lights and unique attractions.
Few could resist them.
Anyone who could pay the entrance fee was gladly welcomed.

Practice: Write three sentences that contain *indefinite pronouns*:

1.

2.

3.

Relative pronouns relate to an antecedent in the sentence and create their own clauses and phrases: who, what, whose, which, that. *Who* is used to refer to people:
Tim asked for the person <u>who</u> was in charge of the carousel.
Gabby, <u>who</u> was feeling rather full from all the food she had consumed, rested by the chattering skeleton.
The spider woman, <u>who</u> scuttled from a web-like structure, turned out to have four arms, two of which were fake.

Practice: Write a sentence that contains the relative pronoun *who*:

1.

Which is used to refer to animals and inanimate things:
The carnival, <u>which</u> had a great many unusual attractions, was in town for two weeks.
The yellow dog, <u>which</u> appeared to be sporting a pair of small wings, ran under the caravan.

 Practice: Write a sentence that contains the relative pronoun *which*:

1.

That is also used to refer to animals and inanimate things:
The horn on <u>that</u> unicorn is slipping.
<u>That</u> is rather strange.

 Practice: Write a sentence that contains the relative pronoun *that*:

1.

What refers to inanimate things, animals and humans:
'Do you know <u>what</u> kind of beast this is?' asked a bystander of Tim.
'<u>What</u> do you think it might be?' wondered Tim.
'<u>What</u> kind of person would know a thing like that?' replied the bystander.

 Practice: Write a sentence that contains the relative pronoun *what*:

1.

Whose also refers to inanimate things, animals and humans:
The unicorn, <u>whose</u> horn was slipping, smiled sadly at Gabby.
'<u>Whose</u> unicorn is this?' Gabby wanted to know.

 Practice: Write a sentence that contains the relative pronoun *whose*:

1.

Demonstrative pronouns are used to identify or point to specific nouns: this, that, these: <u>That</u> man took Gabby's *candyfloss*.

Practice: Write a sentence that contains a demonstrative pronoun:

1.

Recipricol pronouns refer to individual parts of a plural ante-cedent: each other, one another's: Tim and Gabby decided to keep an eye on *each other*.

Practice: Write a sentence that contains a recipricol pronoun:

1.

Reflexive pronouns: these pronouns end with the suffixes -self or -selves and refer to the subject of the sentence or clause in which they are used: *myself, yourself, himself, herself, itself, oneself, ourselves, yourselves, themselves*:
'I hope he doesn't hurt <u>himself</u>,' said Gabby anxiously as she watched the Lizard Man scale the side of the Ferris wheel.

Practice: Write a sentence that contains a *reflexive pronoun*:

1.

Intensive pronouns: these pronouns are spelled the same as reflexive pronouns but function only to emphasize the subject of a sentence, clause or phrase:
The Lizard Man <u>himself</u> slithered down the side of the Ferris wheel.

Practice: Write a sentence that contains an *intensive pronoun*:

1.

Prepositions

Prepositions are words that show relationships between other words such as verbs, nouns and pronouns. Because the preposition overlaps with other parts of speech, especially adverbs and conjunctions, its grammatical classification often depends on where it is placed in the sentence or phrase. For instance, in the sentence, *Giles and Gillian went up the hill*, *up* is a preposition, but in *they climbed up the hill*, *up* is an adverb. Traditionally, the preposition consists of one- or two-syllable words such as *about, above, across, after, against, along, among, around, as, at, before, behind, below, beneath, beside, between, beyond, by, concerning, despite, down, during, except, for, from, in, inside, into, like, near, of, off, on, onto, outside, over, past, since, through, to, toward, under, unlike, until, up, upon, with, without.*

 Practice: Write Three sentences that contain *prepositions*:

1.

2.

3.

Compound prepositions are two prepositions used together as one such as, *in* and *to/into*; *with* and *out/without*; *on* and *to/onto*.

 Practice: Write a sentence that contains a *compound preposition*:

1.

Unlike major word classes such as verbs and nouns, prepositions do not stand alone but need a complement. Typically this is a noun or pronoun: *We will dine at sunrise*; *After the ball* but *before the bat*. However, they may also be other parts of speech: *By then it was over*; *In short, I was afraid*. Prepositions can also be followed by an -*ing* clause: *She deserves a prize for having kept her seat on the bucking bronco ride*. They may also be followed by a *wh-* clause: *For what reason did she do that?* They rarely precede *that* except in some dependent clauses: *I'm sure you were surprised in that you didn't think she could*. Prepositions are not followed by infinitives: *We want to be here next year.* (yes) *We look forward to be here next year.* (no)

Prepositions may be used to express several different relationships: Space and time: *We met outside the Hall of Mirrors at seven o'clock.* Cause and purpose: *Tim bought some more candyfloss for Gabby.* Agent and instrument: *Murdered by an assailant; stabbed with a knife.* The possessive case: *That's one of my arms over there, not yours.* Origin: *Is it really one of a set of six?* Artist: *That looks like the work of the magician.* Representation: *A picture of Winnie came to mind.* Subject: *He told her of his fears.* Make and material: *The arms were made of fake fur.*

Practice: Write seven sentences using one of the relationships described above for each:

1.

2.

3.

4.

5.

6.

7.

In most cases, if the preposition modifies more than one word in the sentence, it does not need to be stated twice: *The carnival stops in Amarillo and Much-Binding-in-the-Marsh.* However, in some sentences the repetition is needed for clarity: *He lived in despair and a caravan/He lived in despair and in a caravan. She lived on charity and a hill/She lived on charity and on a hill.*

Practice: Write a sentence in which the preposition modifies more than one word:

1.

Practice: Write a sentence in which the same preposition is repeated for clarity:

1.

Generally, sentences should not end with a preposition: *What did the murderer do that for?/Why did the murderer do that?* In some cases it is unavoidable: *I bet he was nothing to look at. It hardy bears thinking about.*

Practice: Write two sentences that contain a preposition within the sentence and two that end with a preposition:

1.

2.

3.

4.

You are the grammar detective:

Choose the appropriate words from the following list to complete the three sentences below:

determiners: the, a, an
pronouns: his, who, she, herself, her, something
prepositions: into, through, to, in, as, around, with

Jason went _____ (preposition)_____ (determiner) Ghost Tunnel with his friend, Jinx, _____ (pronoun) thought _____ (pronouns) saw _____ (pronoun) strange _____ (preposition) the cobwebs.

Gabby found _____ (pronoun) unnerved when Tim pointed _____ (preposition) the prostrate woman _____ (preposition) a knife in _____ (pronoun) back.

Ben hears strange noises _____ (preposition) the carousel spins slowly _____ (preposition), and _____ (pronoun) suspicions are aroused when _____ (pronoun) sees ____ (determiner) attendant who appears to be smirking.

Part Two: The Sentence

A sentence is a group of words that expresses a complete thought, feeling, or idea and contains a subject, implied or explicit, and a verb.

Subjects and Predicates

The sentence contains two essential parts: a subject and a predicate. The subject is what or who the sentence is about. The rest of the sentence is called the predicate and contains the verb. The predicate includes one or more clauses and/or one or more phrases: *Laughing nervously,* (phrase) *Jinx and Jason* (subjects) [*rode the ghost train (until it screeched to a halt)*] (clause) [predicate].

 Practice: Write three sentences and identify the *subject* and the *predicate* of each:

1.

2.

3.

Grammar Detective: Turn back to 'The Mystery of the Ghost in the Tunnel' and identify the subject(s) and predicate(s) of two sentences:

1.

2.

Clauses

A clause is a group of words that contains a subject and a predicate and may be independent or subordinate. An independent clause can stand alone as a complete sentence: *Jinx seems nervous, but Jason is anticipating a thrilling ride*. A subordinate (or dependent) clause begins with words that act as subordinating conjunctions which subordinate one or more clauses to the main sentence: *after, although, as soon as, as if, as though, because, before, even if, even though, how, if, in case, in that, inasmuch as, insofar as, lest, no matter how, now that, once, provided (that), since, so that, supposing that, than, though, unless, until, when, whenever, where, wherever, whether, while* and *why*. Subordinate clauses introduce, join and relate the clause to other words in the sentence and cannot stand alone; they must be joined to an independent clause:

Whenever the cobwebs brush Jinx's face, she gives a small scream.

Jason didn't flinch although he felt a bit nervous.

Officer Bloggs came to investigate the circumstances surrounding the missing pair in case foul play was involved.

Jinx screamed because the cobweb stroked her face.

 Practice: Write three sentences that contain one or more *subordinate clauses*:

1.

2.

3.

Subordinate clauses may work as modifiers, subjects, or objects within the sentence:

The ghost tunnel was renowned for its scary effects <u>which made most visitors quake with terror</u>. (<u>modifier</u>)
<u>What Jinx thought she saw</u> may not be what really happened. (<u>subject</u>)
Jinx didn't know why <u>she was so terrified</u>. (<u>direct object</u>)

Practice: Write three sentences that contain (1) a subordinate clause as a modifier (2) a subordinate clause as a subject, and (3) a subordinate clause as a direct object:

1.

2.

3.

Conjunctions

To join independent clauses, use either a coordinating conjunction or a conjunctive adverb. An independent clause can stand alone, or it can be combined with one or more other independent clauses or with one or more subordinate clauses to make a sentence: *Jinx screamed. Jinx screamed* (independent clause)*, but* (coordinating conjunction) *Jason laughed* (independent clause) *when* (subordinator) *a cobweb stroked their faces* (dependent clause). Coordinating conjunctions are words such as *but, or, for, so, yet, nor*. When used as coordinating conjunctions to join two or more independent clauses, they should be preceded by a comma.

Jinx smiles, <u>but</u> Jason sighs as they step off the Ghost Train.

 Practice: Write three sentences that contain two *independent clauses* joined by a *coordinating conjunction*:

1.

2.

3.

Correlative conjunctions, sometimes called parallel conjunctions, are pairs of words or phrases such as: *both–and, either–or, neither–nor, not only–but also, whether–or, just as–so, not–but*. These correlative conjunctions correlate terms within a sentence:

The onlookers were <u>not only</u> intrigued <u>but also</u> anxious. <u>Either</u> Jason and Jinx had imagined it, <u>or</u> something very odd was afoot thought Officer Bloggs as he twirled his moustaches.

Practice: Write three sentences that *correlate terms*:

1.

2.

3.

Grammar Detective: Turn back to 'The Mystery of the Ghost in the Tunnel' and identify five sentences that use at least one conjunction and the kind of clause or clauses it modifies:

1.

2.

3.

4.

5.

Conjunctive adverbs are words such as *however, nevertheless, consequently, furthermore, otherwise, then, therefore, meanwhile, likewise* and *hence*. When used as conjunctive adverbs to join two or more independent clauses, they must be preceded by a semicolon and followed by a comma: *Officer Bloggs asks them a question; <u>however,</u> they do not hear it because of the loud hoot from the departing Ghost Train.*

Practice: Write three sentences that use conjunctive adverbs to join at least two *independent clauses*:

1.

2.

3.

Sentence Forms

There are four different sentence forms: simple, compound, complex and compound-complex. A simple sentence contains one independent clause and may contain one or more subjects and one or more predicates:

The smell of hot dogs (subject) *drifted across the carnival grounds.* (predicate)

The smell of hot dogs and a cool breeze (subjects) *drifted across the carnival grounds.* (predicate)

A cool breeze (subject) *drifted across the carnival grounds and flirted with Officer Bloggs's moustaches.* (predicates)

 Practice: Write three simple sentences and underline the subject and predicate of each:

1.

2.

3.

A compound sentence contains at least two independent clauses and no subordinate clauses:

A distant scream came from the roller coaster; however, it did not distract the attention of the crowd. The small weasel-like man sat down on the grass, but he did not relinquish his umbrella.

 Practice: Write a compound sentence.

1.

A complex sentence contains one independent clause and at least one subordinate clause: *The carnival magically appears in town, unannounced, once every two years* (independent clause) *unless it is engaged elsewhere.* (subordinate clause)

Practice: Write a complex sentence.

1.

A compound-complex sentence consists of at least two independent clauses and at least one subordinate clause: *Everyone in the surrounding countryside tries to visit the carnival* (independent clause); *however, not all are fortunate enough to do so* (independent clause) *because it is only open to those who receive a special invitation* (subordinate clause).

Practice: Write a compound-complex sentence.

1.

Grammar Detective: Turn back to 'The Mystery of the Ghost in the Tunnel' and identify each of the four different forms of sentence: simple, compound, complex and compound-complex:

1.

2.

3.

4.

Sentence Types

There are four types of sentence: declarative, imperative, inter-rogative and exclamatory. Declarative sentences, the most common kind, make statements: *Jinx and Jason are beginning to relish their ordeal. However, no one has yet found an answer to the missing couple.*

 Practice: Write a declarative sentence.

1.

Imperative sentences make commands or requests:
'Stand back!' orders Officer Bloggs.
'Make me!' replies the weasel-like man brandishing his furled umbrella.

 Practice: Write an imperative sentence.

1.

Interrogative sentences ask questions:
'Do you want to be arrested?' asks Officer Bloggs.
'Are you threatening me?' counters the little man.

 Practice: Write an interrogative sentence.

1.

Exclamatory sentences express strong feelings:
'Good grief!' continues the little man, 'I think you are!'
'I am doing no such thing!' is Officer Bloggs's indignant reply.

 Practice: Write an exclamatory sentence.

1.

Grammar Detective: Turn back to 'The Mystery of the Ghost in the Tunnel' and identify one of each of the four sentence types: declarative, imperative, interrogative and exclamatory:

1.

2.

3.

4.

Phrases

A phrase is a group of words that functions as a grammatical unit within a sentence.

There are six typical kinds of phrase: noun phrases, verb phrases, verbal phrases, prepositional phrases, appositive phrases and absolute phrases.

Noun phrases function in the sentence as subjects, objects and complements:

The Ghost Tunnel is a main attraction. (subject)
The police renamed the Ghost Tunnel the scene of the crime. (object)
Screams and cries from its dark interior floated across the carnival grounds. (subject complement)

Practice: Write three sentences that contain *noun phrases*: a subject noun phrase, an object noun phrase and a complement noun phrase.

1.

2.

3.

Verb phrases function in the sentence as predicates:
Curious bystanders have congregated outside the Ghost Tunnel.
The police are still looking for the missing girl.

Practice: Write three sentences that contain a *verb phrase*.

1.

2.

3.

Verbal phrases function in the sentence as nouns or as modifiers but not as verbs. There are three kinds of verbal phrases: gerund, infinitive and participle. Gerund verbal phrases are always used as subjects or as objects: *Asking the bystanders to move, is not a good idea.* *Officer Bloggs insists on <u>asking the bystanders to move</u>.*

Practice: Write two sentences that contain a gerund phrase as a subject and a gerund phrase as an object.

1.

2.

Infinitive phrases, like gerund phrases, usually function as subjects or as objects, but they may also be used as modifiers:
<u>To discover what had happened in the Ghost Tunnel</u> is Officer Bloggs's aim.
His aim is <u>to discover what happened in the Ghost Tunnel</u>.
The onlookers, <u>to ease the tension</u>, begin talking quietly among themselves.

Practice: Write three sentences that contain an infinitive phrase used as a subject, an object and a modifier:

1.

2.

3.

Participle phrases usually modify nouns:
The onlookers, <u>talking quietly</u>, experienced a delicious sense of foreboding.

Practice: Write a sentence that contains a participle phrase.

1.

Prepositional phrases contain a preposition and one or more words:

according to, along with, apart from, as for, as regards, as to, because of, by means of, by reason of, by way of, due to, except for, in addition to, in case of, in front of, in lieu of, in place of, in regard to, in spite of, instead of, on account of, out of, up to, with reference to, with regard to, with respect to and *with the exception of.* These phrases function in the sentence as nouns, pronouns, adjectives, adverbs, or verbs and modify nouns, pronouns, adjectives, adverbs, or verbs.

<u>Behind</u> his hand, he hid a smile.

A crowd of onlookers gathers <u>in front of</u> the Ghost Train.

<u>With the exception of</u> a few stragglers, the crowd forms a tight group.

Officer Bloggs, <u>by means of</u> an expression of stoic disapproval, manages to keep the crowd behind the yellow line.

Practice: Write three sentences that contain different uses of the *preposition.*

1.

2.

3.

Practice: Write three sentences that contain *prepositional phrases.*

1.

2.

3.

Appositive phrases add extra information to the word or words to which they refer:

A policeman, <u>Officer Bloggs</u>, takes charge.

One member of the crowd, <u>a small weasel-like man brandishing a furled umbrella</u>, takes exception to Officer Bloggs's admonitions.

Practice: Write three sentences that contain *appositive phrases.*

1.

2.

3.

Absolute phrases modify the whole sentence and are usually separated from the main sentence by commas:

Jinx, <u>feeling rather perky now that she was out of the tunnel and in the limelight</u>, waves gaily at the crowd.

<u>Not wanting to antagonize the crowd</u>, Officer Bloggs confines his disapproval to facial expressions.

 Practice: Write three sentences that contain *absolute phrases*:

1.

2.

3.

Grammar Detective: Turn back to 'The Mystery of the Ghost in the Tunnel' and identify five sentences with *prepositions* and/or *prepositional phrases*:

1.

2.

3.

4.

5.

Interjections

An interjection is a part of speech that often functions alone rather than as a conventional element of a sentence. The interjection may be one or two words that may stand alone or may appear at the beginning of a sentence. A sentence will remain complete if the interjection is removed. Interjections are often, but not always, used with an exclamation mark to express emotions or commands and are usually capitalized:

'_Wow_! What a great time we've had,' said Tim as they got on the bus.
'_Hey_, isn't that the missing Lizard Man?' asked Gabby as she peered out of the steamy window.
'_Crikey_!' (BrE) exclaimed Tim, 'It is. And he's waving goodbye to us.'

 Practice: Write three sentences that contain three different _interjections_.

1.

2.

3.

You are the grammar detective:

Complete the answers to the following questions by finding the sentence within each mystery. Example:

The Mystery in the Ghost Tunnel

Question: What shoots out of the wall?
Clue: subject and predicate
Answer: 'A skeletal hand shoots out of the wall.'
(sentence # 20)

The Mystery in the Hall of Mirrors

Question: Where do Gabby and Tim take Officer Bloggs?
Clue: subject and predicate
Answer: _____.

Question: How do Gabby and Tim look in the mirrors' reflections?
Clue: two clauses
Answer: _____.
        clause   clause

The Mystery in the Ghost Tunnel

Question: What does Jason ask Jinx to remember?
Clue: conjunction
Answer: _____.

Question: How does Jinx react to the skeletal hand?
Clue: compound sentence
Answer: _____.

The Mystery at the Carousel

Question: What does Emma say as she claps her hands?
Clue: exclamation
Answer: _____.

Question: What is the first carousel animal Emma sees?
Clue: phrase
Answer: _____.

Question: What does Ben do when he sees Officer Bloggs?
Clue: interjection
Answer: _____.

Part Three: Punctuation

Punctuation may be defined as the standard group of symbols or marks used to organize writing into its various components. These symbols or marks include: commas, periods, semicolons, apostrophes, quotation marks, question marks, exclamation marks, colons, dashes, hyphens, parentheses, brackets, slashes, ellipses and emoticons. Using the appropriate punctuation, you, the writer, are able to convey meaning from spoken to written speech, define grammatical elements in the sentence and suggest intonation.

Commas

Commas may be used before coordinating conjunctions, after introductory words, phrases and clauses, to separate items in a series, and to set off non-restrictive and other parenthetical elements. Use a comma before the coordinating conjunctions *and, yet, but, so, for, nor, or:*

The attendant is missing, <u>yet</u> the carousel starts moving.
The animals make noises, <u>but</u> each voice belongs to another.
The noises are loud, <u>and</u> a cacophony fills the evening air.

 Practice: Write three sentences that contain *coordinating conjunctions.*

1.

2.

3.

Use a comma after introductory words, phrases and clauses:
'<u>Yes,</u> there is definitely something fishy going on here,' says Ben (word)
<u>From other carnival venues,</u> a crowd begins to gather, <u>drawn by the gradually increasing noises of the carousel's animals</u> (introductory prepositional phrase and non-prepositional phrase)
<u>Although some faces in the crowd show consternation,</u> most are laughing (introductory clause)
Note: Do not use a comma after an inverted phrase:
<u>With the crowd</u> came a sense of spectacle (*A sense of spectacle came with the crowd*)

Practice: Write three sentences with an introductory word, phrase and clause.

1.

2.

3.

Use a comma to separate items in a series:
The animals are grunting, whistling, clucking, and braying with no regard to vocal ownership.
Note: in British English, the serial comma is often left out, i.e.:
AmEng: *There was a donkey, a hippo, and a chicken.*
BrEng: *There was a donkey, a hippo and a chicken.*

 Practice: Write a sentence that lists a series of items:

1.

Use a comma to set off non-restrictive words, phrases, clauses and other parenthetical elements. If the word, phrase, or clause is restrictive, it is essential to the meaning of the sentence and does not require commas. Non-restrictive words, phrases and clauses provide non-essential, extra, information about a noun or a pronoun and do require commas. To check to see if your word, phrase or clause is non-restrictive, remove the phrase from the sentence and see if the sentence still makes sense:
P. C. Bloggs, <u>the policeman with the large moustaches who had been called to the mystery in the Hall of Mirrors and the mystery in the Ghost Tunnel</u>, arrives on the scene (non-restrictive). *P. C. Bloggs arrives on the scene.*
Use a comma with non-restrictive appositives. Appositives may give added information about the noun or pronoun (non-restrictive) or they may identify a particular noun or pronoun (restrictive):
Ben, <u>who has taken Emma off the carousel</u>, is beginning to enjoy the situation (non-restrictive)
The animal <u>which is clucking like a chicken</u> is the small grey donkey (restrictive)

Practice: Write a sentence that contains a *non-restrictive appositive*.

1.

Practice: Write a sentence that contains a *restrictive appositive*.

1.

Use commas with parenthetical elements:

'We will, <u>I hope</u>, get to the bottom of this mystery,' says Officer Bloggs.
Ben, <u>anxious to get Emma safely off the carousel</u>, lifts her down from the pink hippo.
Emma, <u>however</u>, is dismayed by the move and protests loudly.

Practice: Write three sentences that contain parenthetical elements.

1.

2.

3.

Use a comma to separate coordinate adjectives (two or more adjectives modifying one noun):

Ben's <u>short-sleeved, green</u> shirt matches his eyes.
Cecy's <u>long, black hair</u> is pulled back in a ponytail.
To check to see if you have coordinate adjectives, you may either switch the adjectives or place the word 'and' between them:
Ben's <u>green, short-sleeved</u> shirt matches his eyes.
Cecy's <u>black, long hair</u> is pulled back in a ponytail.

Practice: Write a sentence that contains *coordinate adjectives*.

1.

Use <u>commas</u> to set off contrasting elements:
Emma, <u>unlike her parents</u>, is enthralled with the children's carousel.

The carousel revolves slowly, <u>each animal smiling enigmatically</u>, in the afternoon sun.

 Practice: Write a sentence with a *contrasting element*.

1.

Use commas with geographical names, with dates (in AmEng) and with addresses:

Houston, Texas
56 Meriweather Lane, Much-Binding-in-the-Marsh, Wessex
November 14, 2006

Note: In British English, the date is written with the day, then the month, followed by the year: 14 January 1998 (14/1/1998). In American English, the month comes before the day, followed by the year: January 14, 1998 (1/14/1998).

 Practice: Write a sentence that contains a geographic location, a date and a time.

1.

Note: Unnecessary use of commas may confuse your reader. Do not use a comma between the subject and verb or between the verb and its object:

Emma, clapped her hands (no)
Emma clapped, her hands (no)
Emma clapped her hands (yes)

Do not use a comma after a coordinating conjunction:

Emma clapped her hands, and, Ben scratched his head (no)
Emma clapped her hands, and Ben scratched his head (yes)

Do not use commas with restrictive phrases, clauses, or appositives:

Every member of the crowd <u>who realizes the voices of the animals are mixed up</u> is laughing.
The man <u>who is laughing more heartily than the rest</u> is standing next to the easel.

Do not use a comma in front of the first item in a series or after the last:

All of the animals including the pink hippo, the grey donkey, the chicken, the lamb, and the sly fox were smiling enigmatically.

Grammar Detective: Turn back to the mystery and identify five different uses of *commas*. Write the sentences below:

1.

2.

3.

4.

5.

Inverted Commas (BrE)/ Quotation Marks (AmE)

Inverted commas or quotation marks are a pair of inverted commas and are always used in pairs. British English uses one pair of inverted commas (single quotation marks) with direct dialogue: *'You are my heart's delight,' warbled Officer Bloggs to his beagle, Beckett* (BrE). American English uses two pairs of quotation marks (double quotation marks) with direct dialogue: *"You are my heart's delight," warbled Officer Bloggs to his beagle, Beckett* (AmE).

 Practice: Write a sentence that contains some direct dialogue:

1.

If you are quoting within a quote use double inverted commas for the second quote in BrE and single quotation marks in American English:
Our local newspaper, the <u>Reversible Globe</u>, states: 'All patrons of the Carnival of Grammar have announced that they have "gathered some interesting and unusual information" while perusing its pages.' (BrE)

Our local newspaper, the <u>Reversible Globe</u>, states: "All patrons of the Carnival of Grammar have announced that they have 'gathered some interesting and unusual information' while perusing its pages." (AmE)

In British English, all sentence punctuation goes outside the quotation marks whereas in American English the punctuation goes within the inverted commas:
When you said 'I feel like staying here forever', I understood. (BrE)
When you said "I feel like staying here forever," I understood. (AmE)

Practice: Write a sentence that contains a direct quote:

1.

Use inverted commas/quotation marks with short titles such as chapters in a book and titles of poems, etc.:
'Reversals and Inversions' is the first chapter of <u>The Carnivalesque Uses of The Umbrella</u> by Nora Bhone. (BrE)
"Reversals and Inversions" is the first chapter of <u>The Carnivalesque Uses of The Umbrella</u> by Nora Bhone. (AmE)

 Practice: Write a sentence that contains the title of a short work.

1.

Use double pairs of inverted commas with words used out of context in British English:
One of the side shows features Varooka who is known as "the endless ballerina", for she is able to spin in place for days on end.
Use single pairs of quotation marks with words used out of context in American English:
One of the side shows features Varooka who is known as 'the endless ballerina,' for she is able to spin in place for days on end.

 Practice: Write a sentence that contains a word or phrase that is used out of context:

1.

Full Stops (BrE)/Periods (AmE)

Full stops or periods punctuate declarative and understated imperative sentences and abbreviations. Use a full stop/period to terminate declarative sentences:

I wish we could find out what's going on. Full stops/periods terminate sentences which are commands but not strongly imperative: *Let's find out what's going on.*

 Practice: Write a sentence with terminal punctuation.

1.

Full stops/periods are used with some abbreviations and acronyms: *On an easel in front of the carousel stands a sign with the initials O.O.O. in large purple letters.*

 Practice: Write a sentence that contains an *acronym*.

1.

Use only one period if the abbreviation comes at the end of the sentence: *The carnival opens at 9 a.m. each morning and closes at 10 p.m.*

 Practice: Write a sentence that ends with an *abbreviation*.

1.

Grammar Detective: Turn back to the mystery and find three sentences that use the period in different ways:

1.

2.

3.

Semicolons

Semicolons are used to join independent clauses and to separate items in a series. Use the semicolon to separate phrases or clauses in a list that contains one or more commas; the comma separates individual items within the group whereas the semicolon separates the groups of words:

P. C. Bloggs began twirling his moustaches, which is an indication that he thought he had an idea of what was going on, gazing reflectively at the man who was laughing louder than the rest; and pacing back and forth.

Practice: Write a sentence that contains groups of words that contain commas and are separated by semicolons.

1.

Placement of the semicolon with other punctuation is as follows. Place the semicolon outside the quotation marks:

The sign read 'O.O.O.'; it was intriguing.

Practice: Write a sentence using a semicolon outside quotation marks.

1.

Place the semicolon outside the end of the parenthesis:

The man stands by the easel (the one with the weird grin on his face); he looks very smug.

Practice: Write a sentence that contains a parenthesis and place the semicolon outside the end of the parenthesis:

1.

If the semicolon comes after an abbreviation, use both the period and the semicolon:

P. C. Bloggs read the cryptic O. O. O.; he realized what it meant.

 Practice: Write a sentence that contains an abbreviation in front of a semicolon.

1.

Grammar Detective: Turn back to the mystery and identify two sentences that use the semicolon:

1.

2.

Apostrophes

Apostrophes show possession, form contractions and form some plurals. Use an apostrophe with nouns and indefinite pronouns to show possession and with singular and collective nouns, indefinite pronouns and acronyms: *Emma's pink hippo*; *the crowd's laughter*; *someone's candyfloss*. Use the apostrophe only with plural nouns ending in -s: *the animals' voices*; *the venues' attractions*.

Practice: Write a sentence that contains the possessive of a plural noun ending in -s.

1.

Use the apostrophe and -s for plural nouns that do not end with an -s: *the policemen's approach*; *the children's excitement*.

Practice: Write a sentence that contains a possessive of a plural noun not ending with an -s.

1.

Use the apostrophe on the last word only to demonstrate joint ownership or to make a compound noun possessive: *Ben and Cecy's daughter; the scene of the crime officer's demeanour*.

Practice: Write a sentence that uses the possessive with joint ownership and one that uses the possessive with a compound noun.

1.

2.

Use the apostrophe with each noun for separate ownership: *Ben's or Cecy's apparel; the donkey's and the giraffe's voices.*

Practice: Write a sentence that uses the possessive with separate ownerships.

1.

Use the apostrophe to demonstrate a relationship in time: *an hour's delay; a day's work.*

Practice: Write a sentence that uses the possessive for a relationship in time.

1.

Use an apostrophe to make contractions of words and to signify other missing elements:
'Don't worry,' says Officer Bloggs, 'we'll soon sort this out.'
'Weren't you in the class of '68?' asks one crowd member of another.
Officer Bloggs nods at the sign, 'I'd like to know who's responsible for this.'
*Do not confuse <u>who's</u> (who is or who has) with <u>whose</u> (pronoun): *Whose sign is this?*

Practice: Write a sentence that contains a contraction and one that uses an apostrophe to signal a missing element.

1.

2.

Use the apostrophe to form plurals of letters and words:
Hmmm. I wonder what the <u>three O's</u> mean? P. C. Bloggs asks himself. He twirls his moustache. Yes. That has to be it. No <u>if's, and's or but's</u>.

Practice: Write two sentences that use the apostrophe to form plurals of letters and words:

1.

2.

Grammar Detective: Turn back to the mystery and find three sentences that use the apostrophe to (1) show possession, (2) form contractions and (3) form plurals.

Question Marks

Use a question mark after direct questions such as a command: *Would you please stand back?* Or a declarative: *Isn't it odd?*

 Practice: Write a command in the form of a question:

1.

 Practice: Write a declarative in the form of a question:

1.

Use a question mark with round brackets (BrE)/parentheses (AmE) to query whether the material is correct or not: *The carnival had been coming to town since 1923 (?). Barney B. Braithwaite (?) Bloggs is Officer Bloggs's full name.*

 Practice: Use a question mark to query the validity of the material.

1.

When a question mark is part of the quoted material, it is placed inside the quotation marks; otherwise, it is placed outside: *'Do you have any idea what is going on?' asks Ben imperatively. Will Officer Bloggs be able to answer him?*

Practice: Write a question that is part of a quotation.

1.

Write a question that is not part of a quotation.

2.

Note: Do not use a question mark with indirect questions: *Officer Bloggs wanted to know what was the significance of the sign.*

Exclamation Marks (BrE)/ Exclamation Points (AmE)

Use an exclamation point or exclamation mark after a single word or a group of words for emphasis, with interjections and with strong commands. If the exclamation mark/point comes at the end of a quote within your sentence, do not use a comma after it: *'Amazing! 'This is the strangest thing I've ever heard!' says Cecy as she listens to the noise 'Stand back!'*

 Practice: Write a word, a group of words and a sentence, using exclamation points/marks.

1.

2.

3.

Note: If the exclamation mark/point comes at the end of the sentence, do not use a period.

 Practice: Write a sentence that ends with an exclamation mark/point.

1.

 Practice: Write a quote that uses an exclamation mark/ point within a sentence.

1.

Grammar Detective: Turn back to the mystery and find two different uses of the exclamation point:

1.

2.

Colons

The colon signifies what is to follow such as a series, an example, an explanation, a list, or a quotation. It may also be used to separate bibliographic information concerning city and publisher and to separate hours and minutes: *'Start from the beginning: the animal noises, the letters on the sign, the missing attendant, and the man leaning against the easel. Describe them all to me,' Officer Bloggs tells Cecy. 'It all started at about 12:25,' begins Cecy. 'It's like this: Ben and I decided to let our daughter, Emma, ride on the carousel ...'*

Practice: Write a sentence that introduces a list.

1.

Practice: Write a sentence that contains a reference to a specific time.

1.

Practice: Write a sentence that uses the colon to introduce an example.

1.

Grammar Detective: Turn back to the mystery and find a sentence that contains a colon and identify the type of use:

1.

Dashes

A pair of dashes is used to emphasize and clarify a parenthetical statement within a sentence: *'I am sure I've seen him before – why can't I remember? – somewhere on the carnival grounds,' murmurs Officer Bloggs.*

Practice: Write a sentence that contains a parenthetical element with a pair of dashes.

1.

The single dash signifies a break in thought or tone and sets off an introductory series:
From the carousel came a medley of animal voices – a magnificent cacophony.
Intrigued, amused, apprehensive and titillated – the crowd was all of these.

Practice: Write a sentence that contains a dash to set off a series.

1.

Practice: Write a sentence with a parenthetical element that signifies a break in thought or tone.

1.

Round Brackets (BrE)/ Parentheses (AmE)

Round brackets/parentheses are used to distinguish non-essential matter and to enclose numerals or letters used for lists:

Now, members of the crowd <u>(at least most of them)</u> begin to lose interest. Those who remain are either <u>(1)</u> anxious to find out what has happened or <u>(2)</u> too tired to move on.

 Practice: Write a sentence that contains *parenthetical material.*

1.

 Practice: Write a sentence that uses numerical elements with round brackets/parentheses:

1.

Note: You may use commas, dashes or parentheses to distinguish parenthetical material in your sentences. Remember that each signifies a different degree of emphasis: commas separate elements with little emphasis; dashes separate elements dramatically, with great emphasis; and parentheses often de-emphasize the elements.

Square Brackets (BrE)/ Brackets (AmE)

Brackets or square brackets set off insertions in quoted matter or alterations to quoted matter and replace round brackets/parentheses within round brackets/parentheses:

Officer Bloggs was quoted in the *Reversible Globe* as saying, 'I have never, while working at the Carnivore [sic] of Grammar, seen or heard anything like this.' (Later, the *Reversible Globe* announced that he [Officer Bloggs] showed remarkable acumen in solving the three mysteries at the Carnival of Grammar.)

 Practice: Write a sentence that contains a quotation with material added and a sentence that contains brackets/ square brackets within parentheses/round brackets:

1.

2.

Obliques (Slashes) (BrE)/ Diagonals (AmE)

Use the slash or more formally the 'oblique' in British English and the 'diagonal' in American English to mark line divisions in quoted poetry, to separate alternative terminology, to separate the parts of fractions and to mark divisions in an internet address:

1. *'The carousel went round and round/The animals' faces never frowned.'*

2. *'Upside Down/Inside Out' is the name on the rickety wood roller coaster.*

3. *2/3 of the crowd is now ready to leave.*

4. *www.carnivalofgrammar.com/hippo*

 Practice: Write a sentence that contains two lines of poetry separated by a slash.

1.

 Practice: Write a sentence that uses a slash to separate different terms:

1.

Ellipses

Ellipses are three equally spaced points used to mark an omission from quoted material or to signify hesitation or reflection:

The animals . . . round and round.

I wonder . . . yes, that's it, thought Officer Bloggs as he surveyed the scene.

Practice: Write a sentence that uses ellipsis to signify omitted material:

1.

Practice: Write a sentence that uses ellipsis to suggest hesitation or reflection.

1.

Grammar Detective: Turn back to the mystery and find three sentences that contain three of the following: dash, parenthesis, brackets, slash, ellipsis.

Emoticons

Emoticons, from the word *emotive,* are an electronic form of communication commonly referred to as *smileys.* They are composed of keyboard characters which, when viewed vertically, signify the mood of the sender. Emoticons are not recognized for business or other formal uses. There are many kind of emoticons; the four most common are:

- the smile: ☺ (a colon followed by the right-hand side of a pair of parentheses/round brackets and often converted automatically by the program)
- the frown: ☹ (a colon followed by the left-hand side of a pair of parentheses/round brackets and often converted automatically by the program)
- the wink: ;-)
- the laugh: :-D

 Practice: Write a message that contains two emoticons to a friend who plans on reading the *Carnival of Grammar.*

1.

You are the grammar detective:

Punctuate the following sentences:

Commas: Mysteries mayhem screams and laughter are all part of the carnival of grammar.

Quotation Marks: It's all been very exciting but also a bit scary said Jinx as she and Jason made their way home.

Full Stops/Periods: 'I could have stayed all night,' said Tim as he and Gabby climbed on board the bus Gabby disagreed.

Semicolons: It seemed a good idea screaming corpses always excite the audience.

Inverted commas: Ben and Cecy sang After the Ball was Over to Emma as they drove home.

Question Marks: 'What do you think was the most exciting thing that happened today' Jinx asked Jason.

Exclamation Marks/Exclamation Points: 'Ouch that chicken just pecked me,' shouted Emma.

Colons: 'Let's go over the food you ate hot dogs, pretzels, ice cream, candyfloss and toffee apples,' Gabby said.

Dashes: Tim sighed. 'It's like this I can't resist all those wonderful smells.'

Part 4: Usage

In linguistics, the word 'usage' means the way terms such as accent, pronunciation, spelling, punctuation, words and idioms, are used in a spoken and written language to convey meaning. With this in mind, what follows are some examples and suggestions for use with word sense, homophones, idioms, British and American spelling, terms in grammar, terms in literary criticism and terms in reasoning, beginning with a list of words whose meanings are commonly confused:

above (preposition) over/higher than
accept (verb) take something offered
actual (adjective) current/present
adapt (verb) to adjust to something
adopt (verb) choose and use
advice (noun) recommended opinion or information
advise (verb) seek (AmE) or offer advice
affect (verb) to influence/produce a change in (noun) feeling associated with emotion
agenda (noun) a list of things to do/schedule
aggravate (verb) (not to be confused with irritate)
allow (verb) let someone do or have something
allude (verb) refer to indirectly
allusion (noun) hint, reference to
almost (adverb) nearly, practically
alone (adjective & adverb) without any other person or thing nearby
also (adverb) in addition to/likewise/as well/too
although (conjunction) notwithstanding that, even though
answer (verb) to reply to something; (noun) a response to a question or action

around (preposition) (prepositional adverb) to the other side of revolving around a centre; comparison (coordinating conjunction); time (preposition)

ashamed (adjective) embarrassed

assure (verb) make certain

awake (adjective) conscious/aware

awake (verb) to wake up

back (noun, verb, adjective, adverb) rear part of the body (noun); move backward (verb); located at the rear (adjective); in a reverse direction (adverb)

baggage (noun) suitcases or bags; an impudent woman

bath (noun) bathtub, have a bath (BrE) take a bath (AmE)

bathe (verb) wash in bathtub

become (verb) to suit the appearance or personality; come to be something

begin (verb) start

beside (preposition) next to

besides (preposition) as well as (adverb) moreover

breath (noun) air inhaled and exhaled

breathe (verb) inhale and exhale

cast (noun, verb) an object made by casting metal or other materials; throw energetically

cautious (adjective) careful

change (verb) become or make different

citizen (noun) legal resident

classic (adjective) highest quality, definitive

close (noun) end of a period of time (verb) cover an opening (adverb) tightly (adjective) near, about to happen

clothes (noun, verb) what one wears; dress oneself or another

comprise (verb) make up, consist of something

condition (noun, verb) the state of someone or something; to have an influence on

continuous (adjective) with no interruption

deep (adjective, noun, adverb) extending downwards; the sea; far down

degree (noun) amount or level

desert (verb, noun) leave or abandon; large arid area

dessert (noun) sweet dish eaten after the main course

disable (verb) limit, put out of action

discover (verb) to find, often unexpectedly

distrust (noun, verb) lack of trust; regard with suspicion

double (adjective, adverb, noun, verb) having two parts; twice the amount; twice as large; to make or become double

earth (proper noun, noun, verb) our planet; soil; to ground an electrical device (BrE)

effect (noun, verb) change, cause to happen

electric (adjective, noun) worked by or producing electricity

elicit (verb) provoke or draw forth a reaction

elude (verb) escape or avoid

employ (verb, noun) use or hire; working for someone

ensure (verb) make possible

entrance (noun, verb) way in; fascinate

especially (adverb) particularly

event (noun) occurrence, often important

except (preposition, conjunction) apart from

explicit (not to be confused with implicit) (adjective) clear, definite

farther (not to be confused with further) (adverb, adjective) to a greater distance or extent; more distant

fast (adjective, adverb, verb, noun) suggesting fast movement; rapidly abstain from food; period of going without food

firstly (adverb) to begin with

front (noun, adjective, verb) part facing forward, boldness; situated in or near the front of something; to face something

further (adverb, adjective) a long way or time off

grievous (adjective) very serious

happen (intransitive verb) occur; affect somebody or something

illicit (adjective) illegal

illusion (noun) impression, daydream, chimera

implicit (not to be confused with explicit) (adjective) implied

imply (verb) suggest

infer (verb) come to a conclusion based on reasoning; imply

insure (verb) cover with insurance to protect against risk

journey (verb, noun) to travel somewhere physically or spiritually, a trip somewhere

lastly (adverb) finally

lawyer (noun) someone practising law, a solicitor or barrister (AmE an attorney)

lay (verb) to put something down

lie (verb, noun) recline; say something untrue; falsehood, fib like (preposition) resembling (verb) enjoy

loose (adjective) free; unrestrained

lose (verb) misplace, fail to win

loss (noun) fact of not having something

media (plural noun – use a plural verb) newspapers, television, radio collectively

moral (adjective, noun) what is right or wrong; a lesson, admonition at the conclusion of a story

morale (noun) emotional feelings

near (preposition) close by (adjective) near future (adverb) drawing near (verb) approach

next (adjective, adverb) something close to something else in space or in time

norm (noun) usual behaviour or pattern

normal (adjective) usual, customary

old (adjective, noun) person or object of certain age; often used in the plural sense as with elderly people

order (noun, verb) instruction, neatness, document; to instruct someone to do a certain thing

personal (adjective) individual, private

personnel (noun) people, workers

place (noun, verb) locality, dwelling; put something down on a surface

precede (transitive verb) say or come before something

price (noun, verb) the cost of something; put a monetary value on something

proceed (verb) go forward, begin or continue with action

quick (adjective, noun) fast, nimble; sensitive area such as flesh under nail or deepest emotions

quite (adverb) entirely, rather, nearly (when used of 'not' quite)

real (adjective) authentic, physically existing

reason (verb, noun) think logically; idea behind something, justification

shade (noun, verb) away from the sun, slightly variable colour, window covering, ghost; protect from the sun, darken part of a drawing

sure (adjective, adverb) true; informal for yes

tenuous (adjective) weak, fragile

testy (adjective) irritable

tetanus (noun) bacterial disease

tortuous (adjective) twisting, winding
torturous (adjective) inflicting pain, causing anguish
used to (adjective) familiar with
veer (verb) turn, swerve
voluble (adjective) fluent, vociferous, talkative
voluminous (adjective) capacious, baggy, big
vouch (verb) promise, swear, guarantee
voucher (noun) coupon, ticket
wander (verb) stroll, walk slowly, stray from the point
wonder (verb, noun) speculate; surprise, phenomenon
zebra crossing (noun phrase) pedestrian crossing place in road
    marked by white stripes (BrE); pedestrian crossing (AmE)

Word Sense

Grammar Detective: Fill in the crossword puzzles below to find the correct form of each word. Each answer has two clues!!

(solutions are on page 136–7)

Word Sense # 1

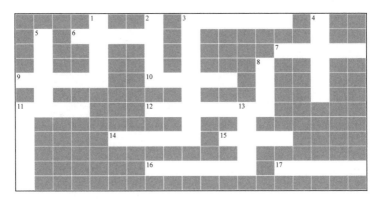

Across
3. a busy one?/he has his own plan for getting it done
6. solitary/existing on one's own
7. facing forward/you've got some!
9. almost but not . . ./are you sure?
10. not dozing/on the ball
11. genuine/is it verifiable?
12. not farthest away/. . . and dearest
14. clean the dog/surround by light and a washcloth
15. throw out the line/don't do this with your pearls
16. safeguard/make it possible, please!
17. subtly allude to/let me suggest it to you gently

Down

  1. where it is/put it over there
  2. in the news/what's going on?
  3. make a bad situation worse/scratching it only does this
  4. dress/get oneself ready for the day
  5. make certain/how can I convince you?
  8. close/who's your neighbour?
 11. because of/argue politely sometimes
 13. 'a lighter . . . of pale'/let's get out of the sun

Word Sense # 2

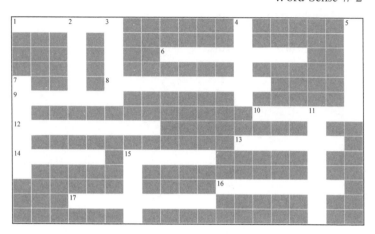

Across

1. seek or offer advice/you tell him, girl!
6. inherent/it's all over the place
8. workers/drones at the office
9. take/do it graciously
10. recommended opinion/go to Google for this
12. twisting, winding/a mountain path is often this
13. emotional feelings/sometimes it needs a boost
14. escape or avoid/hopefully, fox to hound
15. higher than, over/raise body and mind
16. illegal/this kind of behaviour is not allowed
17. made up of/contain all sorts of things

Down

2. protect against risk/keep one safe from penury
3. apart from/other than that
4. speculate/it might require a leap of faith
5. come before/you first!
7. more distant/beyond the woods
11. chimera/is this a fantasy?
15. to adjust to something/"I've grown accustomed to your face"

Word Sense # 3

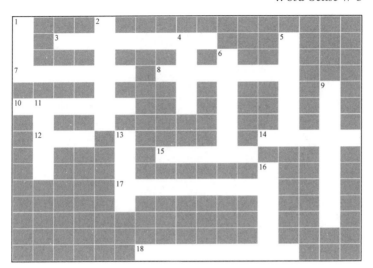

Across

3. private/none of your business!
7. result/do it for a good one
8. other than/as well as tea, I like coffee
10. stroll, meander/let's mosey on down to the river
12. recline/do this when you are tired
14. irritable/you need to calm down!
15. occurrence/could be a life-changing one
17. reference/is that a hint?
18. in the reverse/some tightrope walkers go this way

Down

1. misplace/did Lucy Locket do this?
2. go forward/do this with caution
4. skilled/clever you!
5. put out of action/that should stop it
6. legal resident/allowed to vote
9. inflicting pain/this is agonizing!
11. permit/give the okay
13. lesson/there certainly is something to that tale!
16. reply/you'll need the question first

Word Sense # 4

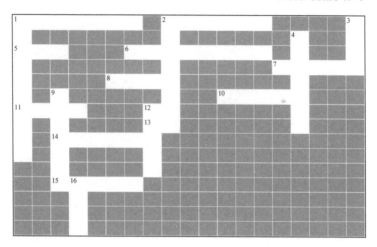

Across

1. coupon/you might need this for a discount
2. amount/you can get one of these at college
5. put down/chickens do it best
6. find/what Columbus did
7. fast/Jack be nimble and ...
8. swerve/you do this in a bumper car
10. start/do this all over again
11. usual pattern/same old thing
14. surrounding/the Ancient Mariner went in this direction
15. our planet/what in the world do you mean?

Down

1. capacious/some dresses are more than others
2. regard with suspicion/I'm not sure about this – something fishy here
3. rear part of body/watch yours, please!
4. trip/could be over land, sea, or air
9. inhale and exhale/we all do it
12. instruction/please place yours
16. as well as/plus is another word for this

Word Sense # 5

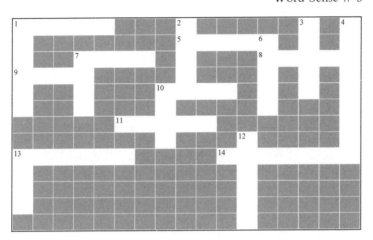

Across

1. narrative/is that a tall one?
5. true/or left?
7. shower, downpour/sometimes it seems never to stop
8. hoofed animal/giddy-up!
9. ceremonial act/some are set in the spring
10. feeble/man, that's not strong!
11. indicate a place/tell me where
13. moved by/bother! a bus just did it
14. largest of the apes/you big lug!

Down

1. floor of a building/first, second or higher
2. put words on paper/go on, be an author!
3. onward/and so on
4. politically motivated soldier/a rebel with a cause
6. belonging to/those naughty kittens lost ... mittens
7. bridle/giddy up and hold on to these tightly
10. seven days/the Beatles' had eight
12. rough sounding/a quadruped with a cough might sound like this
13. period of time/ memories are sometimes buried in this

Homophones

Homophones are words which sound the same but are different in spelling and in meaning. Some homophones have more than one meaning, and because these words sound alike, it is easy to misuse them, especially those people who are learning English:

all ready (adjective) prepared for something
already (adverb) by now

all together (pronoun + adverb) jointly, collectively
altogether (adverb) with everything included

all ways (pronoun + noun) customs, distance travelled
always (adverb) through all past and future time

altar (noun) religious table-like structure
alter (verb) change, adjust

ball (noun) spherical object, often a toy; formal dance
bawl (intransitive verb) cry noisily

bare (adjective) naked, unembellished
bear (verb, noun) support, endure, assume, show, carry; furry mammal

brake (noun, verb) a device for stopping a machine; slow down or stop a machine
break (verb, noun) fragment, separate into pieces; hiatus in activity

buy (verb, noun) purchase; something bought
by (preposition) move past someone or something

capital (noun, adjective) seat of government, principal city of a country; upper case letter; relating to death penalty

Capitol, The (noun) meeting place of United States Congress

cite (transitive verb) quote someone or something
sight (noun) faculty of seeing, vision
site (noun, transitive verb) a place where something happens or
    stands; position something

coarse (adjective) rough, vulgar, tasteless
course (noun) sequence of events, period of time, action
    chosen, direction travelled

complement (noun, verb) something that completes or perfects
    something, full quantity; to add for improvement
compliment (noun, transitive verb) spoken or written praise;
    praise or flatter someone

council (noun) committee, governing group of people
counsel (noun, verb) court lawyer, someone who gives legal
    advice; advise someone

dear (adjective, BrE) expensive
dear (noun, adjective) someone who is loved; a salutation,
    beloved
deer (noun) a forest animal, usually with antlers

discreet (adjective) tactful
discrete (adjective) distinct, separate

eminent (adjective) of high standing
imminent (adjective) about to occur
immanent (adjective) existing within or inherent in something

every day (adjective + noun) each day
everyday (adjective, noun) usual, ordinary; routine occasion
    (AmE)

forth (adverb, preposition) onward, into view; away from
fourth (noun, adjective) one of four parts; position

farther (adverb, adjective) to a greater distance or extent; more
    distant
further (used as a comparative of far) (adverb, adjective) a long
    way or time off; remote in space or time

gorilla (noun) largest of the apes; brute

guerrilla/guerilla (noun) irregular soldier, often politically motivated

hear (verb) distinguish sounds
here (adverb) at this time or place

hoarse (adjective) rough sounding
horse (noun) four-legged animal with hooves

its (possessive pronoun, adjective) indicates possession or relation
it's (pronoun + verb) contraction of 'it is'.

know (verb) understand, be informed about something
no (interjection, noun, adjective) deny or refuse something or someone; voting response; not one person or thing

lead (verb, noun, adjective) guide, be in charge or ahead of; leash; principal one
lead (pronounced 'led', noun) chemical element; fishing line weight

may be (verb + intransitive verb) suggests the possibility
maybe (adverb) perhaps, suggests uncertainty

passed (past tense of pass, verb) transferred, moved by
past (adjective, verb noun, preposition, adverb) period of time gone by; later than a certain time; on the farther side

plain (adjective, noun) simple, not ornate, clear, obvious; large, flat expanse of land
plane (noun, adjective) aircraft, tool for smoothing wood; flat

principal (adjective, noun) most important, fundamental; head, leader
principle (noun) belief, code, rule

rain (noun, verb) precipitation, shower; pour, shower
reign (noun, verb) period of time in power; rule, govern
rein (noun) bridle, restraint

read (verb) understand writing, study
reed (noun) grass plant, musical instrument

right (adjective, adverb) true, approved, usual; properly
rite (noun) ceremonial act, formal procedure
write (verb) put words on paper, create a piece of literature

sight (noun, verb) vision, faculty of seeing, see something
site (noun, transitive verb) a place where something happens or
stands; position something

story (noun) fictional or factual tale or narrative; a lie (as in tall
   story); also used in AmE instead of storey
storey (noun); part of a building where rooms are located on
   one level, also used in AmE

stationary (adjective) not moving, unchanging
stationery (noun) writing materials

their (adjective, pronoun) belonging to an individual or group
   of people or things
there (adverb) indicates a place, activity, or process
they're (pronoun + linking verb) contraction of 'they are'

tail (noun) hindmost part of an animal, someone who follows
   another (informal), refers to a woman (vulgar)
tale (noun) story, lie, as in tall tale
tell (verb) inform, narrate

to (preposition, adverb) indicates direction, forms of infinitive
too (adverb) in addition, more than is needed ·
two (noun) the value of 2

waist (noun) body area between ribs and hips
waste (verb, noun) use something carelessly, weaken; unwanted
   material

weak (adjective) not strong
week (noun) seven days

weather (noun, verb) condition of the atmosphere; survive a
   crisis
whether (conjunction) indicates alternatives

which (adjective, pronoun) introduces a relative clause
witch (noun) someone with magical powers

who's (pronoun + linking verb) contraction of 'who is'
whose (pronoun, adjective) belonging to who or which

your (adjective) belonging to someone
you're (pronoun + linking verb) contraction of 'you are'

Grammar Detective: shade in, or circle, the correct letters to spell the words from the list below. Use the correct form of each word to complete the sentences that follow.

(Solutions are on page 138)

(Solutions are on page 138)

Puzzle #1

O	E	T	D	T	L	T	F	D	D	X	G	S	G	Q
T	B	E	V	A	H	W	A	I	T	F	N	N	W	X
K	E	K	E	P	O	G	W	E	I	L	I	M	E	A
R	V	T	D	A	E	L	I	H	M	R	R	M	A	V
Q	S	E	Y	S	S	W	H	E	E	B	W	D	R	P
Q	B	E	B	D	V	O	N	D	W	R	V	E	P	O
P	Y	M	Y	Q	N	F	L	P	L	A	E	A	Q	K
B	H	O	O	E	V	S	C	R	V	L	H	R	A	E
S	T	N	W	K	H	O	S	F	E	Z	G	Q	U	L
O	N	V	M	A	D	B	M	D	X	E	J	X	C	K
S	T	E	E	L	R	P	S	L	L	M	D	E	I	O
U	P	F	A	O	D	E	I	O	P	G	K	O	A	X
B	S	D	Z	S	O	T	J	J	K	Y	Q	B	T	S
Y	J	O	P	X	B	Y	I	F	G	I	R	L	F	T
X	M	H	J	P	T	N	L	G	R	M	R	P	S	I

dear/deer
led/lead
meat/meet
ring/wring
ware/wear/where
weight/wait
steal/steel

Nigel used to be a _____ little kitten.
The _____ ran through the forest.

Emma took Tomàs's hand and _____ him across the road.
You _____; I'll follow.

The butcher sold fresh _____.
I'll _____ you in the library.

My daughter has a diamond _____.
_____ out the washing before you hang it on the line.

I have a nice collection of ceramic _____.
What will Lisa _____ to the office?
_____ is the library?

I must admit to a little _____ gain
_____ for the bus on that corner.

At that price, it's a _____.
You need to _____ yourself for the upcoming test.

Puzzle #2

V	G	O	N	G	W	D	L	J	W	G	L	P	D	I
B	G	U	J	T	U	E	A	H	E	C	X	A	S	R
U	L	L	O	G	I	E	D	O	A	H	E	N	I	E
C	E	I	L	I	N	G	S	C	T	R	A	R	U	E
Q	V	T	T	H	R	R	U	S	H	N	Z	R	N	D
P	T	I	Z	R	R	R	O	G	E	J	F	I	E	D
C	E	N	R	B	R	L	Y	B	R	D	H	L	B	F
D	C	D	E	A	T	O	W	E	D	W	U	P	M	P
U	R	J	N	R	Y	Z	Q	V	M	T	O	S	K	T
M	R	T	K	V	R	A	G	M	W	O	C	W	D	S
X	I	U	M	H	L	U	V	Z	N	X	Z	T	Y	Q
Y	A	W	J	P	G	L	C	Z	S	N	C	S	O	K
F	H	T	I	D	E	X	A	Q	W	Y	W	E	K	V
N	D	E	E	N	G	N	I	L	A	E	S	U	A	P
V	M	T	U	E	E	T	B	R	I	G	D	G	H	I

ceiling/sealing
guessed/guest
hare/hair
read/reed
toad/towed/
whine/wine
tide/tied
currant/current

Soon, Tomàs will be painting the _____.
First, he is _____ the cracks.

I might have _____ this would happen.
Only you would turn up with an unexpected _____.

Aesop wrote a fable about a tortoise and a _____.
A tortoise has no _____.

A clarinet is a kind of _____ instrument.
How old were you when you learnt to _____?

Which one of you prefers rainy _____?
_____ you live in Texas or in Sussex, it rains a lot during June.

In 'The Wind in the Willows' there is a _____ who lives in a large house.
The battery is dead, so I'll have to have the car _____.

I'm not going to _____ about it.
I'll simply have a glass of _____ when I get home.

Let's meet on the beach at neap _____.
If you're _____ up at that time, let me know.

Hungry Lisa left only a _____ on her plate.
The river's _____ is swift and strong.

Do you really need that last scone?
The baker will _____ his dough before shaping it into a loaf.

Puzzle # 3

I	T	H	D	A	I	G	C	F	D	T	O	O	L	L
F	H	G	U	P	N	D	T	E	N	T	R	S	K	Q
H	R	U	O	P	M	N	W	P	H	N	N	U	N	I
K	E	O	L	V	A	O	E	C	E	I	P	E	O	W
U	W	R	A	T	L	A	F	J	I	K	G	V	W	C
F	A	H	V	L	C	C	A	U	G	H	T	H	W	K
I	O	T	A	E	Z	W	K	Z	T	V	Q	E	E	J
Z	L	E	X	M	X	Z	B	L	A	Y	N	J	C	R
O	F	L	M	Z	K	N	O	A	X	K	L	T	U	R
N	X	P	X	A	Y	Z	K	S	L	V	V	R	C	V
K	I	G	T	V	G	T	B	T	L	T	M	O	X	T
T	E	Z	C	D	W	M	Y	N	C	Y	M	U	G	Y
F	M	T	D	X	R	H	C	L	G	P	Q	X	Z	B
G	F	P	X	B	T	F	P	R	H	I	R	E	H	V
G	L	F	P	N	B	A	J	V	I	Y	U	M	C	X

aloud/allowed
court/caught
higher/hire
knew/new
piece/peace
threw/through

Sometimes, I feel like singing _____ in the library.
I realize that it is not _____.

Lisa presented her client's case in _____.
Lisa certainly _____ the judge's attention.

If you want to make a _____ score, you might need to hire a tutor.
Is that bicycle for _____?

Anyone who _____ Nigel would love him.
I just bought him a _____ collar.

I'll give you another _____ of cake.
I need a little _____ and quiet.

Tomàs _____ the red ball.
_____ the hoop it dropped.

Puzzle # 4

J	E	K	F	J	W	T	L	A	A	P	P	N	L	I
W	L	L	E	A	X	O	E	C	A	R	E	H	A	Y
N	O	T	P	E	T	O	D	E	R	I	A	C	T	O
C	I	R	M	I	P	P	E	M	R	N	R	G	I	B
S	O	B	P	M	S	U	E	F	P	C	N	T	P	M
S	T	A	T	I	O	N	A	R	Y	I	S	U	A	M
P	C	A	E	N	Z	I	I	S	V	P	J	I	C	G
O	O	N	T	C	D	N	C	V	Q	L	O	B	D	F
V	R	O	N	I	C	R	J	H	J	E	M	C	Y	Y
B	P	S	R	I	O	X	V	W	Q	N	D	V	K	G
W	U	D	P	L	N	N	E	T	E	R	C	S	I	D
N	H	A	P	O	U	R	E	T	O	N	K	P	E	C
X	L	B	M	S	T	T	X	R	B	X	A	S	C	N
O	D	X	Z	U	P	I	P	M	Y	I	E	H	G	C
I	Y	Z	Y	D	X	F	G	M	R	F	P	H	I	O

capital/capitol
discrete/discreet
knot/not
pair/pear
paw/poor/pour
peak/peek
stationary/stationery
principal/principle

London is the _____ city of England.

The Texas State _____ is the building in Austin where state legislature takes place.

Please be _____ when you discuss our family's peccadilloes.
These peccadilloes can be placed into _____ categories.

Eventually, I will unravel this _____.
I will _____ lose my patience.

That couple make an odd looking _____.
For dessert, he served a _____ torte.

_____ Nigel is limping.
He injured his _____.
I'll _____ him some cream.

Mount Kilimanjaro's _____ is extremely high.
Pack your bags, and we'll take a _____.

I'll borrow some of my mother's nice _____ to write to Winnie.
Winnie sat _____ in the park.

My _____ complaint concerns the lack of service.
Surely, the main _____ of the bank should be customer service.

Puzzle # 5

```
A  P  C  Z  M  C  X  S  E  A  R  Y  R  E  H
V  X  P  U  F  H  Z  E  N  T  I  C  K  H  R
F  E  L  L  H  E  X  S  N  H  S  A  M  F  F
W  L  Q  A  A  F  B  R  Y  E  R  A  X  P  P
K  Y  W  Z  Y  I  L  U  G  B  P  L  W  D  N
E  B  R  E  A  K  N  O  I  S  L  H  R  A  E
T  S  I  A  W  R  S  C  I  B  A  C  Y  H  U
M  P  R  C  L  J  V  G  V  B  N  T  C  L  X
Z  S  G  A  K  S  H  X  U  U  E  I  W  Y  Q
P  T  M  K  O  T  E  M  G  P  H  W  O  A  A
I  N  Y  Z  R  C  E  E  D  W  D  J  B  D  G
U  U  I  Q  X  X  S  I  T  E  Z  D  M  C  S
H  G  I  K  A  S  F  E  Q  H  M  P  Y  U  X
W  X  G  K  Y  G  U  F  J  L  T  V  I  N  D
Z  D  N  X  R  I  K  E  H  H  F  X  W  Q  L
```

brake/break
coarse/course
plain/plane
sight/site
waist/waste
witch/which

Why don't you _____ before we drive into that ditch!
Please don't _____ the teapot!

The surface still feels rather _____.

I will sand it smooth over the _____ of the morning.

The airport is in _____ view.
The plane is landing now.

What a wonderful _____ that is.
It looks like a good _____ for commercial development.

This skirt feels a little loose in the _____.
That's probably because of all the food you have _____.

Careful, one of those women is a real _____.
Thanks for the warning, now could you tell me _____ one?

British and American Spelling

Some words are spelled differently in British and American English, and some terms also differ. Most words that are spelled differently may be classified under two headings: systemic and non-systemic. Systemic words are those which are part of a group such as the *our/or* group: *colour/color*, or the *re/er* group: *centre/center*; the final *-l* group: *instil/instill*, the *lyse/lyze* group: *analyse/analyze*, and the *ogue/og)* group: *catalogue/catalog*. Non-systemic classification applies to single words or a small group of words such as *gaol/jail* or *cheque/check*. If you are unsure of the spelling of a word, most British and American dictionaries will give you the alternate example. Some words and phrases also differ:

British English/American English

bonnet/hood (car)
boot/trunk (car)
windscreen/windshield (car)
earth/ground (electrical)
petrol/gas (gasoline)
rubber/eraser
£ (pound sterling)/pound (hit, AmE and BrE)
$ (dollar bill) £ (pound sterling)
bill/check (restaurant)
crisps/chips (potato)
chips (potato)/French fries
bum/behind
bum/hobo
subway/underground walkway
underground, tube/subway
pavement/sidewalk

lift/elevator
first floor/second floor
ground floor/first floor
flat/apartment
trousers/pants
knickers/panties, underwear
plus fours/knickers
pissed off, angry/pissed
pissed/drunk
travelling salesperson/solicitor
solicitor/lawyer
barrister/attorney
estate agent/realtor
braces/suspenders
suspenders/garter belt
nappy/diaper
rubbish/trash
rubbish bin/trash can
jam/jelly
jelly/Jello

Idioms

An idiom is a phrase unique to the language and its people, and it is difficult, if not impossible, to understand an idiom by looking at the meaning of each word. Idioms make the language colourful and typical of certain places and people, but for the person who is learning the language, idiomatic sayings can be a challenge because they are not related to words that correspond in meaning: 'Inspector Bloggs simply could not *fathom it out*.' Idioms are not only quite confusing but also easy to misquote, especially those that use prepositions such as the following: *in the creek* (no)/*He's acting as if he's <u>up the creek</u>* (unstable); *around the moon* (no)/*I'm <u>over the moon</u> because I received a pay raise (rise)* (extremely happy); *on the carpet* (no)/*You lied, so don't try and sweep it <u>under the carpet</u>* (cover it up). Many idioms such as *for certain* or *in any case* are not as vivid, and, because their form is fixed, they are easier to use. Other idioms are just as vivid but short and used for certain effects: *get lost! belt up! hold on! stuff it! hang in there!*, etc. Always check the dictionary definition if you are unsure of the idiomatic meaning of words and phrases.

Grammar Detective: Using the numbers that correspond with the letters below, fill in the blanks to find the idioms; then, complete the sentences that follow by adding the appropriate idiom from those you have created.

(Solutions are on page 147)

A B C D E F G H I J K L M N O P Q R S T U V W X Y Z
1 2 3 4 5 6 7 8 9 10 11 12 13 14 15 16 17 18 19 20 21 22 23 24 25 26

‾‾‾‾‾‾‾ ‾‾‾ ‾‾‾‾‾‾‾‾ ‾‾‾‾‾‾‾ ‾‾‾‾‾‾‾
3-1-19-20   13-25   16-5-1-18-12-19   2-5-6-15-18-5   19-23-9-14-5

‾‾‾‾‾‾‾‾‾ ‾‾‾
2-1-18-11-9-14-7   13-1-4

‾‾‾‾‾‾‾‾‾‾‾ ‾‾ ‾‾‾ ‾‾‾‾‾
5-12-5-16-8-1-14-20   9-14   20-8-5   18-15-15-13

‾‾‾‾‾‾‾ ‾‾‾‾‾ ‾ ‾‾‾‾‾ ‾‾ ‾‾‾ ‾‾‾
2-5-20-20-5-18   20-8-1-14   1   19-12-1-16   9-14   20-8-5   6-1-3-5

‾‾‾‾‾ ‾ ‾‾‾ ‾‾‾
23-9-20-8   1   23-5-20   6-9-19-8

‾‾‾‾‾‾‾ ‾‾‾ ‾‾‾‾‾ ‾‾‾‾‾
2-1-3-11-9-14-7   20-8-5   23-18-15-14-7   8-15-18-19-5

‾‾‾‾‾‾ ‾‾‾ ‾‾‾‾‾
1-3-18-15-19-19   20-8-5   16-15-14-4

A B C D E F G H I J K L M N O P Q R S T U V W X Y Z
1 2 3 4 5 6 7 8 9 10 11 12 13 14 15 16 17 18 19 20 21 22 23 24 25 26

‾‾‾‾‾ ‾‾‾ ‾‾‾‾
20-1-11-5-19   20-8-5   3-1-11-5

Now complete the following statements using one of the idioms you have completed for each:

1. It was a tough exam, and I can't believe she finished before I did; that really:

2. I didn't get much for all the time I spent on this project, just a handshake, but I suppose that's:

3. I've had enough rejections; no more shall I:

4. That man is wearing six hats and walking on his elbows; he must be:

5. Looking back, after all my losses, I realize I was:

Now check your idioms against those listed below:

1. different kettle of fish: different from other situations or items in the same class

2. elephant in the room: ignoring the obvious because it's offensive or embarrassing

3. familiarity breeds contempt: seeing too much of one thing or person can lead to revulsion

4. it's a jungle out there: a wild and dangerous situation

5. save the bacon: make thing safe

6. you can't make a silk purse out of a sow's ear: if the prototype is poor, you can't make it better

7. zero hour: when the action begins

8. in the lap of the gods: beyond the control of mortals; up to fate

9. in a pickle: in a tricky situation

10 across the pond: over the Atlantic ocean

11. backing the wrong horse: choosing a loser

12. cast my/your pearls before swine: offer good things or advice to a person who doesn't appreciate it

13. different strokes for different folks: not everyone does thing in the same way

14. takes the cake: (ironic) beats all else

15. jump the broomstick: get married

16. barking mad: as crazy as a rabid dog

17. better than a slap in the face with a wet fish: pretty awful, but not as bad as it could be

Glossary of Terms in Grammar

absolute phrase: absolute phrases modify the whole sentence and are usually separated from the main sentence by commas (see p. 54).

abstract noun: abstract nouns are non-countable and express qualities, concepts and emotions such as: *fear, excitement, nausea, dizziness, exuberance*, etc. (see p. 4).

acronym: a word formed by the first letters of a group of words such as a title, e.g. NASA (National Aeronautics and Space Administration) (see p. 67).

active voice: a sentence in which the subject carries the action (see p. 19).

adjective: a word or phrase that modifies or describes a noun or a pronoun (see p. 25).

agreement: the grammatical construction of a verb and a subject. For regular verbs the 'rule of the one –s' applies (see p. 10).

animate/inanimate noun: animate nouns are nouns that may have a male or female reference: father, boy, mother, girl whereas inanimate nouns name non-living things (see p. 4).

antecedent: a word or a group of words to which a pronoun refers (see p. 32).

appositive: a word or phrase that gives extra information about a noun (see p. 53).

article: the, a, or an (see p. 29).

auxiliary: another word for a helping verb (see p. 10).

case: position or form of a noun or pronoun that describes its relationship with other words in the sentence (see p. 2).

clause: a unit of words within a sentence that contains a subject and a verb and may stand alone as a sentence (see p. 43).

collective noun: nouns that name groups of persons or things: *crowd, audience, group, herd, team*, etc. (see p. 5).

comma splice: an error in punctuation that occurs when two independent clauses are joined with only a comma instead of a conjunction (see p. 45).

common noun: a word that names words that are not proper names (see p. 3).

complement: a word or group of words that complete the verb, subject, or object (see p. 16).

complex sentence: a sentence which contains one independent clause and one or more dependent clauses (see p. 48).

compound–complex sentence: a sentence which contains at least two independent clauses and one or more dependent clauses (see p. 48).

compound sentence: a sentence which contains at least two independent clauses and no dependent clauses (see p. 47).

concrete noun: a noun that is countable and names objects that can be identified through one or more of the five senses (see p. 3).

conjunction: a word or group of words that connects words, phrases, clauses and sentences (see p. 45).

conjunctive adverb: a word that simultaneously modifies a verb or verb phrase and connects sentence elements (see p. 46).

coordinating conjunction: short words that connect other words, phrases, clauses and sentences: and, yet, but, so, for, or, nor (see p. 45).

correlatives: word pairs that link equal sentence elements (see p. 45).

dash: a short horizontal line used as a punctuation mark (see p. 79).

demonstratives: this, that, these and those (see p. 29).

dependent clause: a subordinate clause that cannot stand alone and is connected to the main sentence (see p. 43).

determiner: a word placed in front of a noun (see p. 29).

diagonal (AmE): a slanting line / (see p. 82).

direct object: a noun or noun clause that refers to the subject and verb of the sentence: *Jason blew the train whistle* (see p. 16).

ellipsis: three double spaced points that signal omitted words or sentences from a document (see p. 83).

emoticons: an electronic form of informal communication commonly referred to as *smileys* and consisting of keyboard characters which, when viewed vertically, signify the mood of the sender (see p. 84).

fragment: an incomplete sentence (see p. 10).

full stop (BrE): terminal punctuation (see p. 67).

fused sentence: a sentence lacking the necessary punctuation (see p. xx).

gerund: the –ing form of a verb that functions as a noun (see p. 52).

helping verb: an auxiliary verb that works with a main verb to produce mood, tense or voice (see p. 20).

homophones: words similar in sound, and sometimes in spelling, but carrying different meanings (see p. 98).

idiom: a phrase unique to the language and its people, and it is difficult, if not impossible, to understand an idiom by looking at the meaning of each word (see p. 114).

imperative mood: imperative mood is used to give a command or to state a direct request. Usually, the imperative mood takes the base form of the verb only and does not include the subject: 'Get cracking!' (see p. 18).

independent clause: a clause that is able to stand alone as a sentence (see p. 43).

indicative mood: the indicative mood is used to describe an opinion, to state a fact, or to ask a question (see p. 18).

indirect object: a person or thing towards which the action is directed: 'Jinx gave *Jason* some of her candyfloss.' (see p. 2).

indirect question: a question presented as a statement (see p. 75).

infinitive: the base form of the verb with 'to' (see p. 17).

infinitive phrase: a phrase that includes the infinitive form: 'Emma wanted *to stay* at the carnival' (see p. 52).

interjection: a short exclamation: 'Crikey!' 'Whoops!' (see p. 55).

intransitive verb: a verb that does not take an object (see p. 16).

irregular verb: a verb that is not inflected by adding -d or -ed to the present form to create past tenses (see p. 11).

linking verb: a verb that links the subject and the subject complement (see p. 16).

misplaced modifier: a descriptive word or phrase that does not modify the subject it is meant to (see p. xx).

modal: helping verbs such as may, can, will, shall, must, ought to, need, dare (see p. 20)

modifier: a descriptive word or phrase (see p. 2).

mood: verb forms such as indicative (fact), imperative (command), subjunctive (possibility) used to express a particular attitude (see p. 18).

non-restrictive: extra information that may be omitted from the sentence (see p. 61).

noun: a word or words that name a person, place, or thing (see p. 2).

noun clause: a subordinate clause used as a noun (see p. 43).

parallelism: equal grammatically corresponding statements or words in a sentence or paragraph.

parenthetical element: asides, non-essential words and information usually set off with commas, dashes, or round brackets/ parentheses (see p. 61).

participle: verb form that is used to form tenses such as 'was singing' or 'has sung' and may also be used as an adjective (see p. 10).

passive voice: the direct object in the sentence becomes the subject: *The bus tickets* (subjects) *were bought by Tim and Gabby* (see p. 19).

perfect tense: the verb tense is formed by the verb 'have' to show temporal relationships and may be present perfect, past perfect or future perfect (see p. 13).

period (AmE): terminal punctuation (see p. 67).

phrase: a group of words punctuated as a sentence that lacks either a subject and/or a verb (see p. 51).

predicate: the part of the sentence that is not the verb (see p. 42).

predicate adjective: describes the subject of a sentence (see p. 16).

predicate noun: identifies the subject of a sentence (see p. 16).

prepositions: words that show relationships between other words such as verbs, nouns and pronouns (see p. 37).

reflexive pronoun: pronouns that end with the suffixes *-self or -selves* and refer to the subject of the sentence or clause in which they are used: *myself, yourself, himself, herself, itself, oneself, ourselves, yourselves, themselves* (see p. 36).

regular verb: a verb that is inflected by adding –d or –ed (see p. 10).

relative clause: an adjective clause introduced by a relative pronoun (see p. 34).

relative pronoun: a noun substitute such as *who, whom, whose, that, which, whoever, whomever, whichever* that often introduces subordinate clauses (see p. 34).

restrictive: a word, phrase or clause that is essential to the meaning of the sentence and requires no commas (see p. 61).

run–on sentence: a sentence that lacks punctuation (see p. xx).

split infinitive: the interruption of an infinitive by another word or words: '*To happily stay* at the carnival another few minutes is what Emma wanted' (see p. 17).

subject: a noun or noun substitute to which the predicate refers (see p. 42).

subordinate clause: a clause that depends on the main clause and begins with a subordinator (see p. 43).

synonym: a word close to or the same in meaning as another.

syntax: the grammatical arrangement of words, phrases and clauses.

systemic or non-systemic classification of spelling: systemic classifies groups of words such as colour/color (the *our* group); centre/center (the *re* group); instil/instill (the final *l* group); analyse/analyze the (*lyse/*group); and catalogue/catalog (the *og(ue)* group). Non-systemic classification applies to single words or a small group of words such as gaol/jail or cheque/check (see p. 112).

tense: the form of the verb that signifies time (see p. 12).

transitions: any unifying word, phrase, sentence or paragraph that links the meaning of writing.

transitive verb: a verb that takes a direct object (see p. 16).

verb: a word that indicates action or being (see p. 10).

word sense: the correct usage of the word given its meaning(s).

Glossary of Terms in Literary Criticism

allegory: a style of writing in which the characters and events are acted out by human, animal, or mythical characters whose actions are symbolic of a deeper meaning, often spiritual, moral, or political such as John Bunyan's *Pilgrim's Progress*.

alliteration: a poetic or literary effect achieved by the uses of the same or like sounding consonants as in 'On the bald street breaks the blank day.' (Tennyson, *In Memoriam*)

antonym: a word opposite in meaning as in 'hot'/'cold'.

assonance: similar vowel sounds in stressed syllables that end with different consonant sounds: 'The bows glided down, and the coast/Blackened with birds took a last look/At his thrashing hair and whale-blue eye;/The trodden town rang its cobbles for luck.' Dylan Thomas, 'Ballad of the Long-Legged Bait'.

ballad: a simple narrative of an exciting or dramatic episode in verse form to be sung or recited, such as Oscar Wilde's 'The Ballad of Reading Gaol'.

blank verse: poetry written in iambic pentameters that do not rhyme such as Milton's *Paradise Lost* and many of William Shakespeare's works.

comedy: a form of drama that aims to amuse and ends happily, such as Shakespeare's *All's Well That Ends Well*.

couplet: two lines of verse with similar end rhymes: 'For never was a story of more woes/Than this of Juliet and her Romeo.'

denouement: the final unravelling of the plot in dramatic fiction; the solution of the mystery; the explanation or outcome.

detective story: a novel or short story involving a crime, often murder, committed by an unknown perpetrator and solved by a detective, such as Conan Doyle's Sherlock Holmes or Agatha Christie's Miss Marple, through his or her powers of ratiocination.

deus ex machina (god from the machine): the use of some unexpected and improbable event or power in a story or play, to make things turn out right.

dramatic irony: hidden meaning in the character's words of which the speaker is often unaware but the audience is, such as Sir Peter Teazle in *School for Scandal*, who doesn't know his wife is behind the screen when he is talking about her.

dramatic monologue: a poem such as Robert Browning's 'Porphyria's Lover' and T. S. Eliot's 'The Love Song of J. Alfred Prufrock', in which the lines are delivered by a single speaker into whose character the reader gains indirect insight as he or she addresses an imaginary audience.

dramatic poetry: poetry that takes the form of a play such as Shakespearian dramas.

elegy: a lyric poem expressing sadness of the deceased, such as 'Lycidas', Milton's pastoral elegy on the death of Henry King.

epic poetry: often historical in theme, focusing on the lives and actions of great men and women, or on historical events in a country, such as Virgil's *Aeneid* and Homer's *Iliad*.

existential sentence: a sentence stating something exists, usually comprise of 'there', a form of the verb 'be' and an indefinite noun phrase: 'There was a young lady from Ghent ...'

farce: a comic play based on gross incongruities, coarse wit, or horseplay to evoke laughter that focuses less on plot and character than on exaggerated and improbable situations, such as Alan Bennett's *Habeas Corpus*.

figurative speech: intentional departure from the literal to the figurative in order to bring freshness and strength to the meaning; to describe through analogy, and to illustrate or discover similarities in otherwise dissimilar subjects: 'She flew like a bird to the arms of her love.'

first-person narrator: the character in the work who tells the story through the first person, such as the 'I' in Charles Darwin's *Voyage of the Beagle*.

flat character: a term first used by E. M. Forster to describe a character built around a single quality or idea, such as Sherlock Holmes.

free verse: poetry lacking a regular metre or rhyme scheme such as many twentieth and twenty-first-century works, including T. S. Eliot's 'The Waste Land'.

homonym: a word that has the same sound and spelling as another, but differs in origin and meaning: rest/rest (repose/remainder).

homophone: words that sound the same as one or more other words but are different in meaning and sometimes in spelling: whole/hole, foul/fowl.

hubris: excessive pride and insolence that usually leads to the downfall of a protagonist in a dramatic tragedy as, for example, the overweening ambition of Macbeth.

hyperbole: a figure of speech in which deliberate and obvious exaggeration is used, such as 'I'm so hungry, I could eat a horse.'

iamb (iambus): a metrical foot consisting of an unstressed syllable followed by a stressed syllable: 'Come <u>live</u> with <u>me</u> and <u>be</u> my <u>love</u>' (Marlowe).

iambic pentameter: the most common metre/meter in English poetry. Each line consists of five feet (pentameter), each containing an unstressed syllable followed by a stressed syllable (iambic): 'The <u>curfew tolls</u> the <u>knell</u> of <u>parting day</u>' (Gray's *Elegy*).

imagery: words used to conjure mental pictures; the connection of images with a literary work: 'Let us go then, you and I /When the evening is spread out against the sky/Like a patient etherised upon a table' (T. S. Eliot, 'The Love Song of J. Alfred Prufrock').

irony: words that refer to the recognition of a reality that is different from appearance: 'You picked a fine time to leave me Lucille', sings the abandoned husband in the country and western song when the rest of his life is falling apart.

lyric poetry: subjective poetry utilizing imagination, melody and emotion to create a single, unified impression, such as Wordsworth's 'Daffodils', currently the most widely used form of poetic expression in Britain and the United States.

metonymy: a figure of speech in which an attribute or part of something is used to represent the thing itself, such as 'top brass' for military officers, or 'the crown' for the queen.

metre/meter: the recurring rhythmic pattern in poetry as determined by stressed and unstressed syllables.

narrative: an account usually in prose but also in verse of a real or a fictional event or sequence of events such as Alan Sillitoe's novel, *Saturday Night and Sunday Morning*.

nemesis: unbeatable enemy often bringing about destruction; in literature what occurs when a character's past actions cause his or her downfall or death.

novel: a book-length narrative; new or unusual.

ode: a short lyric poem unified with one theme and purpose that celebrates a person, object, or event, such as Keats's 'Ode on a Grecian Urn', or Shelley's 'Ode to the West Wind'.

omniscient point of view: used in fiction to describe the third-person point of view in which the character is capable of seeing, knowing and telling whatever he or she wishes.

oxymoron: a self-contradictory combination of two or more such as 'bitter-sweet' or 'jumbo shrimp': 'I will complain, yet praise;/I will bewail, approve;/And all my sour-sweet days/I will lament and love' (George Herbert).

paradox: a phrase or statement that seems absurd or contradictory, but is often true: 'The Child is father of the Man' (Wordsworth).

pathetic fallacy: a pejorative term first used by John Ruskin to describe the tendency to credit nature with human emotions and create 'a falseness in all our impressions of external things', such as, 'They rowed her in across the rolling foam – /The cruel, crawling foam.' (Charles Kingsley)

personification: discourse in which animals, plants, elements of

nature and abstract notions are given human attributes such as
Shelley's 'bask in heaven's blue smile'.

plot: the pattern or plan of events in a play, short story, poem, or
novel and the organization of characters and incidents to elicit
suspense and curiosity in the reader or audience.

prose: language that is not poetry.

prosody: the study of poetic structure.

rhyme scheme: the pattern in which the rhyme sounds occur in a
poem.

short story: a relatively brief fictional prose narrative ranging from
about 500 to 15,000 words.

simile: a figure of speech in which the similarity between two
usually disparate objects is directly expressed through such words as
'like' and 'as': 'My love is like a red, red rose' (Shakespeare);
'A dungeon horrible, on all sides round,/As one great furnace
flames . . .' (Milton).

soliloquy: a speech delivered by a character in a play or other work
while he or she is alone and intended to convey the character's
thoughts and ideas to the audience such as Hamlet's famous soliloquy that begins 'To be, or not to be'.

sonnet: a lyric poem usually of 14 lines and iambic pentameters that
most generally follows one of three rhyme schemes: Petrarchan,
Spenserian, or Shakespearean.

stanza: a recurrent grouping of two or more lines of a poem in
terms of length, metrical form and, often, rhyme scheme.

stream-of-consciousness: a type of psychological novel taking as its
subject matter the uninterrupted, uneven and endless flow of the
stream of consciousness of one of its characters such as the novels of
Virginia Woolf and James Joyce.

synonym: a word similar in meaning to another: eccentric/odd,
weird, wacko, etc.

tragedy: in drama a particular kind of play such as *Hamlet*; in poetry
and fiction, especially the novel, a work that reflects the tragic
sense of a life such as Theodore Dreiser's novel *Sister Carrie*.

trope: a figure of speech involving a 'turn' or change of sense – the use of a word or phrase in a figurative, rather that literal, way.

verse: a unit of language in metrical form, often rhyming.

Glossary of Terms in Reasoning

Making your point reasonably and persuasively increases the chances that your argument will be accepted. The two most common structures used in argument are inductive and deductive reasoning. Inductive reasoning is probably the most common form of argument as most of us use this approach on a daily basis. It is also used frequently in science where it is called the 'scientific method'. Central to inductive reasoning is the *inductive leap*, a generalization which is based on a certain amount of gathered evidence: *Every time Ben eats more than five hot dogs, he becomes sleepy.* (Inductive leap: *Ben should eat fewer hot dogs*.) Be careful to give equal balance to the evidence and claim. If, for instance, you implied that everyone should eat fewer than five hot dogs, your claim would be too large for the amount of evidence. A well-balanced argument based on inductive reasoning does not result in positive proof, but it can render a probable, believable conclusion or induction. In deductive reasoning, the *premise* is the central element. This kind of argument is based on a structure known as a *syllogism*, which contains a major premise, a minor premise and a claim. The premise or principle may be stated or assumed to be true:

> Major premise: *Everyone who goes to the carnival has a good time.*
> Minor premise: *Gabby is going to the carnival.*
> Claim: *Gabby will have a good time.*

A syllogism with an assumed or unstated premise is called an 'enthymeme': *Gabby is going to the carnival, and she's going to have a good time.* (assumed premise). If you use an *enthymeme* for your argument, it is important that your audience agrees with the stated premise or you might end up with a faulty syllogism: *Jinx ᵔ Texas, so she must like fried chicken.* Perhaps not all Texans ᵔ ᵉd chicken!

Fallacies are lapses in reasoning that are often brought about by faulty premises or poorly presented issues and evidence. Below are some of the most widely recognized fallacies:

- Ad hominem: a personal attack on an opponent is order to draw attention away from the issues: *The man who founded the carnival is unfit to be the mayor because he has a wooden leg.*
- Begging the question: a circular argument that assumes the question has already been answered: *We need more side shows at the carnival.* It needs to be proved first that the need exists.
- Post hoc fallacy (post hoc, ergo propter hoc/after this, therefore caused by this): assumes that because one incident happened after another, it must have been caused by the first: *We should not have more side shows at the carnival. The last one we added, 'Donatello and His Dozing Donkeys', was not a huge success.*
- Non sequitur (it does not follow): attempts to connect two or more unrelated concepts as if they were related: *If there were more side shows at the carnival, the rain would ease off.*
- Either–or fallacy: asserts that a complex situation can have only two possible results: *If we don't add more side shows at the carnival, people will stop attending because of lack of interest.*
- Hasty generalization: conclusion of the argument is based on misleading or scanty evidence: *Tim couldn't find the bobbing duck, so he knew someone had run off with it.*

Suggested Reading

W. H. Auden (1963). *The Dyer's Hand*. London: Random House.

The Oxford Advanced Learner's Dictionary of Current English. Oxford: Oxford University Press.

The Oxford Companion to the English Language. Oxford: Oxford University Press.

Solutions

Solution to the Mystery in the Hall of Mirrors

There is no corpse! Gabby and Tim do see a woman who is lying on the floor, and she does have a knife in her back, but it is the woman from the House of Horrors next door. She plays the role of the 'Screaming Corpse' and ends her part by running outside with a knife from the Fake 'n' Fun toy booth stuck in her back and collapsing on the ground. Tim sees her in the many contorting mirrors which reflect the open door of the Hall of Mirrors. Impelled by the thought of imminent danger or perhaps even death, she disappears as if by magic behind his back to return to the House of Horrors.

Solution to the Mystery in the Ghost Tunnel

Fleur and her companion bend down to avoid the skeletal hand that shoots out of the wall in the bend in the tunnel. Jinx glances around with trepidation. The two seem to have been swallowed up by the tunnel; however, it is not what she thinks! Officer Bloggs observes the situation and comes up with an idea. He desists in twirling his moustaches, and, to prove his theory, he enters the tunnel's dark mouth and leads out the terrified friends who have been sitting in the dark for several minutes, and the mystery is solved: when the Ghost Train came to a halt, only the section in which Jinx and Jason were seated emerged from the tunnel due to a malfunction in the tracks.

Solution to the Mystery at the Carousel

The attendant, a thwarted disc jockey and an amateur stand-up comedian, has cunningly mixed up the carousel sound tape of the animals' voices to confuse his patrons and left behind a cryptic message on the easel that reads 'O.O.O.': out of order. He grins maliciously and watches Ben and Cecy's confusion with great glee. Officer Bloggs, however, looks from the sign to the man who stands behind the easel and smiles enigmatically as he twirls his moustaches. 'I think we can get to the bottom of this. The reason for this cacophony is,' he points at the grinning man, 'this attendant is a sly fox who enjoys playing tricks on his unsuspecting patrons.'

Solutions to the sentences:

The Mystery in the Hall of Mirrors

Question: Where do Gabby and Tim take Officer Bloggs?
Clue: subject and predicate
Answer: sentence # 22

Question: How do Gabby and Tim look in the mirrors' reflections?
Clue: two clauses
Answer: sentence # 6

The Mystery in the Ghost Tunnel

Question: What does Jason ask Jinx to remember?
Clue: conjunction
Answer: sentence # 34

Question: How does Jinx react to the skeletal hand?
Clue: compound sentence
Answer: sentence # 21

The Mystery at the Carousel

Question: What does Emma say as she claps her hands?
Clue: exclamation
Answer: sentence # 9

Question: What is the first carousel animal Emma sees?
Clue: phrase
Answer: sentence # 6

Question: What does Ben do when he sees Officer Bloggs?
Clue: interjection
Answer: sentence # 32

Solutions to punctuation:

commas: Mysteries, mayhem, screams, and laughter are all part of the carnival of grammar.

quotation marks: 'It's all been very exciting but also a bit scary,' said Jinx as she and Jason made their way home.

full stops/periods: 'I could have stayed all night', said Tim as he and Gabby climbed on board the bus. Gabby disagreed.

semicolons: It seemed a good idea; screaming corpses always excite the audience.

inverted commas: Ben and Cecy sang 'After the Ball was Over' to Emma as they drove home.

question marks: 'What do you think was the most exciting thing that happened today?' Jinx asked Jason.

exclamation marks/exclamation points: 'Ouch! That chicken just pecked me!' shouted Emma.

colons: 'Let's go over the food you ate: hot dogs, pretzels, ice cream, candyfloss, and toffee apples,' Gabby said.

dashes: Tim sighed. 'It's like this – I can't resist all those wonderful smells.'

Solutions to crossword puzzles

#1

across:
3/agenda
6/alone
7/front
9/quite
10/
11/real
12/nearest
14/bathe
15/cast
16/ensure
17/imply

down:
1/place
2/media
3/aggravate
4/clothe
5/assure
8/next
11/reason
13/shade

#2

across:
1/advise
6/immanent
8/personal
9/accept
10/advice
12/tortuous
13/morale
14/elude
15/above
16/illicit
17/comprise

down:
2/insure
3/except
4/wonder
5/precede
7/farther
11/illusion
15/adapt

#3

across:
3/personal
7/effect
8/besides
10/wander
12/lie
14/testy
15/event
17/allusion
18/backward

down:
1/lose
2/proceed
4/adept
5/disable
6/citizen
9/torturous
11/allow
13/moral
16/answer

#4

across:
1/voucher
2/degree
5/lay
6/discover
7/quick
8/veer
10/begin
11/norm
14/around
15/Earth

down:
1/voluminous
2/distrust
3/back
4/journey
9/breathe
12/order
16/also

#5

across:
1/story
5/right
7/rain
8/horse
9/rite
10/weak
11/there
13/passed
14/gorilla

down:
1/storey
2/write
3/forth
4/guerrilla
6/their
7/rein
10/week
12/hoarse
13/past

Solutions to word search puzzles:

Puzzle # 1

```
+  +  +  D  T  L  T  +  +  +  G  +  G  +
+  +  E  +  A  H  W  A  I  T  +  N  N  W  +
+  E  +  E  +  +  G  W  E  +  +  I  +  E  +
R  +  T  D  A  E  L  I  H  M  R  R  +  A  +
+  S  E  +  +  +  +  +  E  E  +  W  D  R  +
+  +  E  +  +  +  +  +  +  W  R  +  E  +  +
+  +  M  +  +  +  +  +  +  +  E  A  +  +
+  +  +  +  +  +  +  +  +  +  L  +  R  +  +
+  +  +  W  +  +  +  +  +  E  +  +  +  +  +
+  +  +  +  A  +  +  +  D  +  +  +  +  +  +
S  T  E  E  L  R  +  +  +  +  +  +  +  +  +
+  +  +  +  +  +  E  +  +  +  +  +  +  +  +
+  +  +  +  +  +  +  +  +  +  +  +  +  +  +
+  +  +  +  +  +  +  +  +  +  +  +  +  +  +
+  +  +  +  +  +  +  +  +  +  +  +  +  +  +
```

(across, down, direction)

DEAR (13, 5, S)
DEER (4, 1, SW)
LEAD (7, 4, W)
LED (11, 8, SW)
MEAT (10, 4, NW)
MEET (3, 7, N)
RING (11, 4, NE)
STEAL (2, 5, NE)
STEEL (1, 11, E)
WAIT (7, 2, E)
WARE (4, 9, SE)
WEAR (14, 2, S)
WEIGHT (10, 6, NW)
WHERE (8, 3, SE)
WRING (12, 5, N)

Nigel used to be a *dear* little kitten.
The *deer* ran through the forest.

Emma took Tomàs's hand and *led* him across the road.
You *lead*; I'll follow.

The butcher sold fresh *meat*.
I'll *meet* you in the library.

My daughter has a diamond *ring*.
Wring out the washing before you hang it on the line.

I have a nice collection of ceramic *ware*.
What will Lisa *wear* to the office?
Where is the library?

I must admit to a little *weight* gain.
Wait for the bus on that corner.

At that price, it's a *steal*.
You need to *steel* yourself for the upcoming test.

Puzzle #2

```
+ + + + G + D + + W + + + D +
+ + + + + U + A + E + + A + R
+ + + + + + E + O A H E + + E
C E I L I N G S C T R A + + E
+ + + T + + + U S H + + R N D
+ T I + + + R + + E + + I E +
+ E N + + R + + + R D H + + +
D + + E A T O W E D W + + + +
+ + + N R + + + + + + + + + +
+ R T + + R + + + + + + + + +
+ I + + + U + + + + + T + +
+ A W + + + C + + + + S + +
+ H T I D E + + + + + + E + +
+ D E E N G N I L A E S U + +
+ + + + + E + + + + + G + +
```

(across, down, direction)

CEILING (1, 4, E)
CURRANT (9, 4, SW)
CURRENT (8, 12, NW)
GUESSED (5, 1, SE)
GUEST (13, 15, N)
HAIR (2, 13, N)
HARE (11, 3, SE)
READ (11, 4, NE)
REED (15, 2, S)
SEALING (12, 14, W)
TIDE (3, 13, E)
TIED (4, 5, SW)
TOAD (10, 4, NW)
TOWED (6, 8, E)
WHINE (11, 8, NE)
WINE (3, 12, SE)

Soon, Tomàs will be painting the *ceiling*.
First, he is *sealing* the cracks.

I might have *guessed* this would happen.
Only you would turn up with an unexpected *guest*.

Aesop wrote a fable about a tortoise and a *hare*.
A tortoise has no *hair*.

A clarinet is a kind of *reed* instrument.
How old were you when you learned to *read*?

Which one of you prefers rainy *weather*?
Whether you live in Texas or in Sussex, it rains a lot during June.

In 'The Wind in the Willows' there is a *toad* who lives in a large house.
The battery is dead, so I'll have to have the car *towed*.

I'm not going to *whine* about it.
I'll simply have a glass of *wine* when I get home.

Let's meet on the beach at neap *tide*.
If you're *tied* up at that time, let me know.

Hungry Lisa left only a *currant* on her plate.
The river's *current* is swift and strong.

Do you really *need* that last scone?
The baker will *knead* his dough before shaping it into a loaf.

Puzzle # 3

```
+ T H D + + + + + D T + + + +
+ H G U + + + + E + + R + + +
+ R U O + + + W P H + N U + +
+ E O L + + O E C E I P E O +
+ W R A + L A + + + G + W C
+ + H + L C C A U G H T H W +
+ + T A E + + + + + + E E +
+ + + + + + + + + + + N + + R
+ + + + + + + + + K + + + +
+ + + + + + + + + + + + + + +
+ + + + + + + + + + + + + + +
+ + + + + + + + + + + + + + +
+ + + + + + + + + + + + + + +
+ + + + + + + + + H I R E + +
+ + + + + + + + + + + + + + +
```

(across, down, direction)

ALLOWED (4, 7, NE)
ALOUD (4, 5, N)
CAUGHT (7, 6, E)
COURT (15, 5, NW)
HIGHER (10, 3, SE)
HIRE (10, 14, E)
KNEW (11, 9, NE)
NEW (12, 3, SE)
PEACE (9, 3, SW)
PIECE (12, 4, W)
THREW (2, 1, S)
THROUGH (3, 7, N)

Sometimes, I feel like singing *aloud* in the library.
I realize that it is not *allowed*.

Lisa presented her client's case in *court*.
Lisa certainly *caught* the judge's attention.

If you want to make a *higher* score, you might need to hire a tutor.
Is that bicycle for *hire*?

Anyone who *knew* Nigel would love him.
Last week, I bought him a *new* collar.

I'll give you another *piece* of cake.
I need a little *peace* and quiet.

Tomàs *threw* the red ball.
Through the hoop it dropped.

Puzzle #4

```
+  +  K  +  +  W  T  L  +  +  P  P  +  L  +
+  +  +  E  A  +  O  E  +  +  R  E  +  A  +
N  O  T  P  E  T  +  +  E  +  I  A  +  T  +
+  +  +  +  I  P  +  +  +  R  N  R  +  I  +
S  +  +  P  +  +  +  +  +  P  C  +  +  P  +
S  T  A  T  I  O  N  A  R  Y  I  S  +  A  +
P  C  A  +  +  +  +  I  +  +  P  +  I  C  +
+  O  +  T  +  +  N  +  +  +  L  +  +  D  +
+  +  O  +  I  C  +  +  +  +  E  +  +  +  +
+  +  +  R  I  O  +  +  +  +  +  +  +  +  +
+  +  +  P  +  +  N  E  T  E  R  C  S  I  D
+  +  A  P  O  U  R  E  T  O  N  K  P  +  +
+  L  +  +  +  +  +  R  +  +  A  +  +  +  +
+  +  +  +  +  +  +  +  +  Y  I  E  +  +  +
+  +  +  +  +  +  +  +  +  R  +  P  +  +  +
```

(across, down, direction)

CAPITAL (14, 7, N)
CAPITOL (2, 7, NE)
DISCREET (14, 8, NW)
DISCRETE (15, 11, W)
KNOT (12, 12, W)
NOT (1, 3, E)
PAIR (13, 12, SW)
PAW (4, 3, NE)
PEAK (12, 15, N)
PEAR (12, 1, S)
PEEK (6, 4, NW)
POOR (1, 7, SE)
POUR (4, 12, E)
PRINCIPAL (10, 5, SW)
PRINCIPLE (11, 1, S)
STATIONARY (1, 6, E)
STATIONERY (1, 5, SE)

London is the *capital* city of England
The Texas State *Capitol* is the building in Austin where state legislature takes place.

Please be *discreet* when you discuss our family's peccadilloes.
These peccadilloes can be placed into *discrete* categories.

Eventually, I will unravel this *knot*.
I will *not* lose my patience.

That couple make an odd looking *pair*.
For dessert, he served a *pear* torte.

Poor Nigel is limping.
He injured his *paw*.
I'll *pour* him some cream.

Mount Kilimanjaro's *peak* is extremely high.
Pack your bags, and we'll take a *peek*.

I'll borrow some of my mother's nice *stationery* to write to Winnie.
Winnie sat *stationary* in the park.

My *principal* complaint concerns the lack of service.
Surely, the main *principle* of the bank should be customer service.

Puzzle # 5

```
+ + + + + + + + E + + + + E +
+ + P + + + + E + T + + K + +
+ + + L + + + S + + S A + + +
+ + + + A + + R + + R A + + +
+ + + + + I + U + B P + W + +
E B R E A K N O + S L H + + +
T S I A W + + C I + A C + H +
+ + R + + + + G + + N T C + +
+ + + A + + H + + + E I + + +
+ + + + O T + + + + H W + + +
+ + + + + C + + + W + + + + +
+ + + + + + S I T E + + + + +
+ + + + + + + + + + + + + + +
+ + + + + + + + + + + + + + +
+ + + + + + + + + + + + + + +
```

(across, down, direction)

BRAKE (10, 5, NE)
BREAK (2, 6, E)
COARSE (6, 11, NW)
COURSE (8, 7, N)
PLAIN (3, 2, SE)
PLANE (11, 5, S)
SIGHT (10, 6, SW)
SITE (7, 12, E)
WAIST (5, 7, W)
WASTE (13, 5, NW)
WHICH (10, 11, NE)
WITCH (12, 10, N)

Why don't you *brake* before we drive into that ditch!
Please don't *break* the teapot!

The surface still feels rather *coarse*.
I will sand it smooth over the *course* of the morning.

The airport is in *plain* view.
The *plane* is landing now.

What a wonderful *sight* that is.
It looks like a good *site* for commercial development.

This skirt feels a little loose in the *waist*.
That's probably because of all the food you have *wasted*.

Careful, one of those women is a real *witch*.
Thanks for the warning, now could you tell me *which* one?

Solutions to idioms puzzles:

idioms solutions: 1/14; 2/17; 3/12; 4/16; 5/11

Index